Landscaping for the Mid-Atlantic

Terry Wallace

Schiffer Publishing Ltd

4880 Lower Valley Road Atglen, Pennsylvania 19310

Landscaping for the Mid-Atlantic

Terry Wallace

Dedication

This book is dedicated to my grandmother, Estelle Kleckner, and my Dad, Guy Thornton. They introduced me to the joy of gardening and the wonders of nature. Patiently sharing their great knowledge of plants and gardening, they allowed me the freedom to experiment—even when the result was a crooked row of Gladiolus straggling across the front lawn. My life has been enriched immeasurably by the passion they inspired in me.

Other Schiffer Books on Related Subjects
Fences, Gates, & Walls, by Ashley Rooney
Fire Outdoors: Fireplaces, Fire Pits, and Cook Centers, by Tina Skinner & Melissa Cardona
Paver Projects: Designs for Amazing Outdoor Environments, by Melissa Cardona
Designs for Garden Paths, by Heidi Howcroft
Garden Ornaments and Antiques, by Myra Yellin Outwater & Eric B. Outwater

Designed by John P. Cheek
Cover design by Bruce Waters
Type set in Aurora Cn BT/Adobe Jenson Pro

ISBN: 978-0-7643-2700-1
Printed in China

Published by Schiffer Publishing Ltd.
4880 Lower Valley Road
Atglen, PA 19310
Phone: (610) 593-1777; Fax: (610) 593-2002
E-mail: Info@schifferbooks.com

For the largest selection of fine reference books on this and related subjects, please visit our web site at
www.schifferbooks.com
We are always looking for people to write books on new and related subjects. If you have an idea for a book please contact us at the above address.

This book may be purchased from the publisher.
Include $3.95 for shipping.
Please try your bookstore first.
You may write for a free catalog.

In Europe, Schiffer books are distributed by
Bushwood Books
6 Marksbury Ave.
Kew Gardens
Surrey TW9 4JF England
Phone: 44 (0) 20 8392-8585; Fax: 44 (0) 20 8392-9876
E-mail: info@bushwoodbooks.co.uk
Website: www.bushwoodbooks.co.uk
Free postage in the U.K., Europe; air mail at cost.

Contents

Acknowledgments

I am grateful to landscape architects Richard Lyon and Laura Miller, whose work is the basis for this book. It has been my privilege to work with these two fine design professionals for many years. I have seen, first hand, the care and creativity they bring to every project and their total commitment to helping each client find the design that fulfills their dreams.

I would also like to recognize the landscape crews of Wallace Associates, Inc., who are responsible for implementing the vision of our clients and designers. They work hard, often under adverse conditions, to create the landscapes pictured in this book.

I acknowledge with gratitude the many families who have allowed me the privilege of working with them to develop their personal gardens. I sincerely hope the process has been as satisfying for them as it has been for me.

Last, but not least, I could not have illustrated this book without the cooperation of the many clients of Wallace Associates Inc., who graciously allowed me to photograph and publish their private outdoor spaces. A sincere thank you to all the homeowners, both those listed here and those who wish to remain anonymous, whose landscapes were photographed for this publication. I am very grateful to them.

Frank and Sandra Baldino
Ken and Kathy Boehl
Bob and Peggy Bradbury
Brian and Lolly Carlson
Pamela Freytag
Rod and Ann Gualtieri
Bettina Jenney
John and Debbie Kollmeier
Richard Szumel and Sonia Kotliar
Stephen and Catherine Marvin
Donald J. Puglisi
Nancy and Scott Sherr
Rita Thomas
Philip and Gillian Timon

Introduction

Landscaping for the Good Life

When I began working as a landscape designer in 1976, what passed for landscaping was often a fringe of evergreen shrubbery across the front of a house. Many of those plants were clipped and tortured into bizarre shapes. There might be a shade tree or two, maybe even a lilac bush in the *yard*. But a *garden*, with outdoor rooms, water features, furnishings and spectacular plantings, was the province of grand estates. Like many outdated ideas, this concept of landscaping has changed. Today, a fabulous garden is recognized as a rich source of satisfaction and pride within the reach of most homeowners.

The purpose of this book is to encourage you to think of your outdoor spaces in a different way. The most enjoyable gardens are designed very much like the interior of a house. They have spaces for the activities of everyday life, as well as those for parties and special occasions. There is a well thought-out circulation pattern, so that you can move from one area to another in a logical flow. And they are decorated with pleasing elements, just as you decorate your rooms with lovely fabrics and artwork.

When treated in this way, a garden becomes an extension of your living space. It reflects and enhances your lifestyle. Some outdoor spaces are designed to surround and enfold you, providing a sense of comfort and intimacy; others open up to sweeping vistas, drawing attention to the vast panorama of nature. The formality of balanced elements is pleasing to some, while others enjoy the mystery of meandering paths and secret gardens or the sunny, unstructured character of a wildflower meadow, alive with birds and butterflies.

Are you faced with a newly built home on a tract of barren land? Perhaps your house is surrounded by an outdated landscape, one that is overgrown and in decline. Such large-scale situations may seem overwhelming. On the other hand, maybe you're ready for a change of lifestyle or you're bored with your surroundings and you want more excitement, more fun, more function in your landscape. Large project or small, there is bound to be space for developing some wonderful features. Depending on your taste and desire, those features might include a rippling pond, a serene meditation garden, or perhaps a potager with an abundance of vegetables, fruit, and flowers.

In my thirty years in the landscape industry, I have worked with hundreds of families, each with a unique vision and budget. When there is a desire, there is always a way to create a very special and personal garden, no matter the size of the space or the bank account. It is an exciting process—full of anticipation, challenges, and rewards. Of course it's nice if you can afford to call in a landscape

Inside or out, a garden is a source of pleasure in every season. This early spring view from a window contrasts the strong silhouette of an American black walnut with the soft green foliage and white bells of a Carolina silver bells. Although the walnut will be one of the last trees to leaf out in the spring, mature trees such as this are very valuable in the landscape. They provide vertical volume, structure, and shade. Black walnuts, common native trees of the Mid-Atlantic region, produce a chemical that inhibits the growth of many plants within their root zone.

architect and installation crews and have it all done professionally in a short time. Whether that is an option, or whether you will do the planning and installation yourself, the first question is: *"Where do I start?"*

I have always encouraged my clients to start by searching their hearts to discover what attracts and excites them. Within the pages of this book, you may find inspiration in the outdoor living spaces others have created. As you tease out your own personal vision, there are many decisions to be made. Will your garden be shady or sunny, active or quiet, private and secluded, or open to grand vistas? Would you enjoy elements of all of the above? Whatever you decide upon, be aware that the final picture will change. For, if there is one immutable fact about every garden, it is that change will take place.

A garden is dynamic. Every feature is influenced by time, the elements, and the traffic to which it is exposed. Materials such as stone and brick are chosen for garden construction, for their ability to withstand sun and rain, freezing and baking, while growing more beautiful with age. They are materials that fit into our traditional garden image. Gradually mellowing and blending with the surroundings, they take on many characteristics of the native environment.

Plant growth, development, and decline contribute to dramatic and constant change. One of the most commonly made mistakes in designing a garden is underestimating mature plant sizes. Even professional landscape designers struggle to place plants so that they create a pleasing picture when young, and still fit into the allotted space as they grow to maturity. This book includes photos of gardens at various stages of development and times of the year, to help you visualize the changes that will take place from month to month and over time.

Work and family obligations have required me to make several moves over the years. As a result, I have created my personal gardens in Pennsylvania, New Jersey, and Delaware. With each move, I left behind a beloved garden and looked forward to the creation of a new one. I gladly left some plants behind and never used them again, while others, such as hostas and Siberian iris, I use over and over. I discovered, by trial and error, the materials, spaces, and construction methods that work best. I found that a garden can develop very quickly and that there is great joy, and hard, but satisfying work in the planning, creation, and maintenance of a new landscape.

The lessons learned in my personal gardens have been extremely helpful in my career as a garden designer. The greatest challenge for me has been guiding clients past their pre-conceived notions and helping them envision and articulate what would bring them the greatest satisfaction in their personal space. An investment in a well-planned landscape returns many years of pleasure. I hope these chapters will help you to discover and create what best suites your needs—and just as importantly your dreams—as you plan your garden.

This book is my way of sharing my thoughts and experience with those who are contemplating the exciting prospect of creating a garden of their own. These are real gardens, cultivated, lived in, and enjoyed by homeowners in the Mid-Atlantic region. Some may not appeal to your tastes or fit the contours of your plot, but among them you will find a wealth of ideas. Take what appeals to you and get started on the great adventure of creating your personal and private garden.

A swimming pool occupies much of the space at the back of this city property. The sparkle of water creates an inviting scene, even in early spring before temperatures encourage taking a dip. This is a landscape designed for an active family to enjoy together.

The gentle patter of a waterfall adds to the enjoyment of a small pond. Boulders, expertly placed by the landscape architect, create a natural appearing water feature that brings magic to this garden. It takes a trained eye to place boulders so that they appear to have occurred naturally.

This circular deck was designed to accommodate a mature tree. Lush plantings enhance the cool, welcoming appearance of the outdoor living space. Existing trees contribute an established appearance to a new garden. They deserve protection during construction and landscaping.

Kids need their own outdoor space. Tucked into a corner of the property, this is a spacious, safe and comfortable playground. It is in easy view of the windows so Mom and Dad can keep an eye on the activities. Nearby garage storage space makes for easy clean up of balls and sports gear at the end of the day.

9

Who can resist following a trail through a shady grove? Pea gravel is a comfortable and easily maintained paving material for an informal garden path, and it keeps feet clean and dry in all kinds of weather. An occasional raking and weed control is all that's needed to maintain the surface.

A formal garden is very appealing, with its sense of order and balance. A comfortable circulation path leads through this estate garden. The landscape becomes less formal as it moves away from the stately home. Features are appropriately sized for the architecture of this large property.

A gracious entrance to a country home features a fountain and antique benches. This newly installed garden looks a bit bare now, but in a short time the plantings will give it an established appearance. Plantings that look full at installation will most likely become overgrown in time.

In early spring, a perennial border shows a bit of color, a foretaste of the masses of flowers that will bloom later in the season. The foliage texture and shades of green make the garden interesting, until it reaches its peak of bloom.

Fast growing Doublefile Viburnum (*Viburnum plicatum tomentosum* 'Mariesii') were planted three years ago as sturdy thirty-inch plants from five gallon containers. They quickly grew to screen a view, as they were intended to do. This variety of Viburnum is carefree and offers the benefits of healthy foliage, lovely flowers in late spring, bright berries through the summer, and purple tinted, yellow fall foliage.

A whimsical invitation suggests the many pleasures of an herb garden. Sharing garden delights is half the fun. Herbs are highly favored among hobby gardeners for their ease of cultivation and their many uses.

Growing food is a satisfying aspect of gardening. Vegetables and herbs are usually grown in a garden set aside for that purpose, but can easily be grown in containers or blended with ornamental plantings in beds.

Sweeping flowerbeds give a warm and colorful welcome to this Maryland country home. By combining flowering shrubbery, annuals, and perennials, the homeowner insures a constant array of bloom throughout the growing season.

Stone walls terrace a sloping site to create a gentle transition to this stately Pennsylvania farmhouse. The wide brick path, flanked by flower beds, leaves no doubt as to which is the front door.

Shading the parking court, these trees are valuable in the heat of summer. The airy blooms of Japanese pagoda trees (*sophora japonica*) add to the cooling picture when they bloom in late July and August.

A small garden set into a large bluestone terrace interrupts the expanse of pavement, providing seasonal interest and defining space and circulation. The terrace is in use spring, summer, and fall as the family dining room, with space enough for neighborhood gatherings and large parties.

Chapter One

A Sense of Place

Many of us have a garden intertwined with our memories. It is important to honor our memories as we design our own gardens. The European heritage of this homeowner is reflected in a pea gravel courtyard, stone columns, and iron gates open to the perennial stroll garden.

Many of us have a garden intertwined with our memories. Even city dwellers like a friend of mine, who grew up on New York's lower east side, have memories of gardens that brought meaning to their lives. Whether of Central Park splendor or a fragrant lilac next to Grandmother's back door, reminiscence is an important tool for designing your garden It is one of many ways in which our landscape comes to have meaning for us. The emotional connections between you and your surroundings are the soul of the garden.

Some of us enjoy duplicating the essential qualities of a remembered garden, while for others a special plant is all it takes to kindle precious memories. A vine covered pergola, the crunch of a gravel path, the music of a wind chime…all may stir memories and feelings in us. Whatever your dream garden looks like, the emotion it evokes is a critical consideration in your design. And that is why you are the expert on what is right for you.

The garden is part of your home. It is a bridge between the man-made world of architecture and the natural world. Inside our homes we have moved away from the idea of setting aside spaces to be decorated and maintained just for special visitors. So, too, have we moved away from the concept of the landscape as mere decoration for the enjoyment of neighbors and those passing by. Your garden is meant to have meaning for you and your family…to be lived in and experienced every day of the year.

If you work with a professional designer, communicate your desires clearly so that your emotional needs are met when your garden becomes a reality. Sometimes designers get so caught up in their own creative process that they tune out your ideas. If you think this is happening, it's time to be assertive about your vision. You are the one who will live with the outcome for many years.

The emotional impact of the garden is often described as *a sense of place*. The most wonderful and inspiring gardens each have a well-defined sense of place—a place remembered or familiar in some way; a place that evokes a feeling of belonging. If you grew up in the Plains states, for example, a plot of grasses waving in the sunlight may suggest a comfortable and familiar place for you. You will likely feel more at home with wide-open spaces than with woodsy enclosures. To those who grew up on the coast of Maine, rugged boulders and gnarled pine trees may look just right. When planning the garden, think about the impact of each component on the goal of creating this sense of place. It will be different for different people, but there are certain elements, such as reflecting pools and disappearing paths, that cause predictable responses resulting from our shared human past.

A garden, like any work of art, is simply a collection of objects. The arrangement of those objects, their color, texture, size and character, will determine the way you and others respond to the garden. Visualize three containers: a two-foot tall, rectangular vessel, glazed brilliant cobalt blue; A simple terra-cotta pot encrusted with mineral deposits and moss, its rim chipped; a graceful cast iron urn, comparable in size to the other two containers, but ornate in design. All serve the same function, but each creates a different picture, a different mood. Visualize an appropriate garden setting for each of them. Which, if any, of those scenes calls to you?

How does a garden create a mood? The forms—open and expansive or inward facing and protective; the colors—soft and serene or bold and energetic; the decorative elements; the selection of materials—all help to weave a spell. If you are still not sure how gardens suggest a specific mood, look at two familiar examples. The English country garden with its jumble of colorful flowers, perhaps contained by a picket fence and entered by way of a rose covered arch, suggests an energetic mood very

different from the Japanese tea garden. In the latter, textures and shades of green, gently curving stone walks, trained plants, and strict placement of elements create a quiet, contemplative ambiance. Think about gardens that appeal strongly to you. What are the elements that draw you to them? What is the mood they create?

In the city, a garden can be an island of serenity…a place to escape the traffic, crowds, and high-tech intrusion. Can you imagine vine-covered walls surrounding a private space, while the gentle splash of a fountain deadens the clamor of the street? A shade tree completes the sense of privacy and enclosure, its overlapping patterns of leaves blocking out the view of surrounding structures. Plantings of rich, dark evergreens contrast with airy ferns. A comfortable bench and perhaps a beloved piece of sculpture and there you have it—a refuge from a busy, noisy world.

In another vision, a swimming pool may occupy the center of attention. Broad brick and stone steps provide transition from an expansive dining terrace adjoining the house. Banks of bright red roses add splashes of color as they define the spaces. The views open out over paddocks, where horses graze peacefully. This is an area that bespeaks movement, activity. It sets the scene for large social gatherings, with plenty of room for the caterers to work—a different mood for a different homeowner.

A wonderfully evocative landscape feature is the beckoning path. With the promise of surprise at every turn, it invites exploration. Who can resist the open gate leading to—who knows where? Perhaps it is a primeval urge we inherited from our adventurous ancestors that makes a meandering trail so irresistible to our exploration. And if the path ends in a secluded grove, we may linger to reflect upon the memories and imaginings brought to mind by our stroll through the garden.

Are you beginning to form a mental picture of your garden? As I will continue to emphasize, a garden is an expression of your style and personality. It can be accessible and welcoming, bright and colorful, or deep, dark, and mysterious. The best thing about a garden is that you don't have to choose. Even a small garden can accommodate play, humor, fantasy and fun, and still have space set aside for moments of quiet reflection. In the very first stages of design, consider your cherished garden memories, dream big dreams, think about landscapes that have moved you, visit public gardens, and gather all your ideas. Then move on to the next step—making it all work.

Dramatic containers reinforce the old world feeling of the landscape. Frequent travelers, the owners bring back artifacts to personalize their garden and remind them of their times abroad.

This historic fireplace issues a warm invitation to gather around the fire. Outdoor firepots and fireplaces act as a magnet to pull family and friends together on cool evenings. Marshmallows anyone?

The gentle enclosure of a pergola adds a vertical dimension to the landscape and evokes a vision of exotic gardens, dreamed or visited in reality.

A rose covered arbor leaves little doubt that you are entering a special place. In this case, it is the lovingly tended potager of a couple who are organic vegetable and fruit growing hobbyists.

Providing a gradual transition from house to swimming pool, this tree-shaded terrace is a breezy place to relax on a warm summer day. Lunch on the terrace is the perfect prelude to a refreshing dip.

A meadow can be a reminder of the freedom of youth, when such a landscape represented an opportunity for exploration and exuberant play. A meadow planting can reduce maintenance over a large tract or it can fill a sunny corner with its lively forms and colors.

A custom made iron fence and gate is an attractive way to enclose a garden, keeping pets in and unwanted intruders out. Fences and enclosures have been an integral part of the garden aesthetic throughout history.

The light fragrance and bold colors of phlox remind us of long, carefree summer days. This old fashioned flower graced many gardens of the past.

Pigs galore lend a personal touch to this garden. A sparkling water feature adds interest to the bluestone seating and dining terrace overlooking lawns, stroll paths, and a nature preserve. Sculpture and special features set a garden apart and express the unique interests and tastes of the owners.

This informal planting creates a subtle division between two properties. It allows for borrowed scenery and an expansive view while demarking the actual boundaries of the properties.

A vivid pool is surrounded by plantings and outbuildings to give a sense of enclosure and intimacy. The desire for a private space is very common and is particularly desirable in a neighborhood setting.

This pool, set in a country property, opens to expansive views. Since the surrounding land is part of this estate, the owners can enjoy their views and still have a sense of privacy.

The beckoning path is an irresistible invitation to further exploration. What is around the next corner? Perhaps the path ends in a shaded grove with a bench for a moment of quiet contemplation.

An open gate issues an invitation to wander down this garden path. Who would guess that this is a city garden with neighboring houses nearby? The design creates a sense of place very different from its surroundings.

A dramatic entrance invites visitors to an authentic re-creation of a prosperous Pennsylvania farmstead, complete with barn and outbuildings and a unique "homestead ruins" enclosing an outdoor fireplace and terrace overlooking a large pond.

These rudbeckia are native plants that may contribute to a sense of place for those who grew up seeing their bright blooms decorating roadsides and meadows.

25

A sweeping staircase leads from the pool to this elegant suburban house. Both house and landscape are successful in their functionality as well as in their expression of the owner's taste.

An all-American welcome greets visitors to a comfortable family home set in an urban neighborhood.

A sculptural dog rests in the shade of a covered terrace. When used discreetly, sculpture personalizes a garden and sets it apart from the commonplace.

Chapter Two
A Garden That Works

Aside from adding beauty and value to your home, a garden has work to do. Planning each element with an eye to its overall functioning is one way of achieving an enjoyable and sustainable landscape. That is why it's important to design and install in an orderly process, such as: grades and drainage, traffic flow, materials, infrastructure, floors and walls, sun and shade, features and focal points, furnishings and plantings. By following such a process, you avoid discovering that you need to run an electric line beneath the terrace, just as the last brick is set in place. You steer clear of costly changes during and after installation. Time spent on planning can save much frustration and avoids wasted time and money.

When a garden works as it should, we don't notice its functional elements; they only come to our attention if something goes wrong or is missing. A few functional considerations are drainage, traffic flow, grade transitions, soil retention, lighting, and irrigation. Trees and shrubs act as functional elements by cooling, directing traffic, screening views, or providing shelter from the elements.

Drainage is a key factor in the success of any landscape, so start by considering the path water will take around structures and through your garden. Water can be a destructive force or a wonderful asset. It is worthwhile to take the time to manage it effectively. If you are already aware of water problems—a damp basement or standing water in low areas—you need the services of a landscape architect or drainage specialist to help you plan a surface water management system. Cutting corners on this aspect of the landscape can lead to years of annoying problems, dead plants, and even damage to the structure of your home.

Directing water into a dry stream or underground drainage system can control surface runoff damage. Proper grading of a gentle slope spreads runoff over a wide area. This sheet drainage allows more of the water to percolate into the soil and helps to eliminate "washouts." Remember, water is a powerful force. It can do great damage if not managed effectively.

A rain garden captures the runoff from a large asphalt driveway. This garden is an effective way to deal with surface water drainage. Rain gardens are gaining wide use by homeowners and municipalities as a way to manage storm water and purify ground water.

It's not simply a matter of directing surface runoff onto the street or the property next door. Most municipalities have laws restricting this. With more and more land covered by impermeable surfaces, run-off is becoming a serious issue. One solution developed to keep and manage water within the boundaries of a property is the rain garden. Homeowners and municipalities are creating special gardens with a permeable sub-strata and plantings that thrive in a moist environment. Surface run-off

is directed into these areas, where it percolates into the ground water system. The plantings and soil layers remove pollutants from the water as well as containing it within the boundaries of the property. Ground water resources are recharged instead of running off into streams.

Rain gardens have gained popularity in recent years. With widespread development comes more impermeable coverage of the soil. Storm water rushes off these surfaces, causing small stream flooding, washouts, and loss of ground water. Rain gardens are landscaped beds designed to capture storm runoff and return it slowly to underground reservoirs (see illustration and list of appropriate plants). They are gaining acceptance as a means of water management for both homes and businesses.

Rain Gardens

A rain garden consists of a shallow depression designed to accumulate runoff and allow it to percolate slowly into the ground water. It is placed so that it will collect water from downspouts and paved surfaces. The soil in the rain garden is mixed with compost and sand to allow infiltration. A mulch layer is also helpful. The collection area is planted with moisture tolerant plantings, creating an attractive landscape bed. It will need to be maintained like any bed, but many of the moisture tolerant plants are robust growers that, when established, will crowd out most weeds and require little care.

Benefits of Rain Gardens

A rain garden has benefits for the homeowner, the community, and the environment. It is a solution to dealing with runoff within the boundaries of a property, helping to eliminate washouts and soggy lawns. Many contaminates are removed as the water percolates through mulch and soil, so it is clean when it returns to the ground water. Rain gardens help with flood control by slowing the rush of water into storm sewers, small streams, and drainage channels. By recharging ground water, rain gardens help to assure a clean supply of water for future use and keep streams healthy at the same time. Rain gardens are simple projects that most homeowners can do themselves, with great potential for improving the environment.

To learn more about rain gardens, visit The Brooklyn Botanical Gardens website (BBG.org) and look under Gardening>Garden Design>Rain Gardens. Other helpful websites are raingardennetwork.com and consciouschoice.com.

Typical Rain Garden Plants

Trees

Red Maple	*Acer Rubrum*
Serviceberry	*Amelanchier canadensis*
River Birch	*Betula nigra*
Sweet Gum	*Liquidamber stryaciflua*
Weeping Willow	*Salix babylonica*
Swamp Cypress	*Taxodium distichum*

Shrubs

Buttonbush	*Cephalanthus occidentalis*
Sweetpepper Bush	*Clethera alnifolia*
Redtwig Dogwood	*Cornus alba 'Siberica'*
Dwarf Fothergilla	*Fothergilla gardenii*
Winterberry	*Ilex verticillata*
Doublefile Viburnum	*Viburnum plicatum tomentosun*

Perennials, Ferns, and Grasses

Goat's Beard	*Aruncus dioicus*
Astilbe	*Astilbe arendsii*
False Turtlehead	*Chelone lyonii*
Joe Pye Weed	*Eupatorium maculatum*
Meadow Sweet	*Filipendula ulmaria*
Daylily	*Hemerocallis cvs.*
Hosta	*Hosta cvs.*
Japanese Iris	*Iris ensata*
Iris siberica	*Siberian iris*
Cardinal Flower	*Lobelia cardinalis*
Meadow Lobelia	*Lobelia syphilitica*
Creeping Jenny	*Lysamachia nummularia*
Ostrich Fern	*Matteuccia struthiopteris*
Owsego Tea	*Monarda didyma*
Sensitive Fern	*Onoclea sensidilis*
Royal Fern	*Osmunda regalis*
Candelabra Primrose	*Primula japonica*
Guinea Hen Flower	*Fritilleria maleagris*
Summer Snowflake	*Leucojum aesticum*
Carex spp	*Carex pendula, Carex stipata.*

MULCH LAYER

AMENDED SOIL

After grading and water management, traffic flow is the next function in the planning process. A can of marking paint is an invaluable tool in planning circulation systems. Mark out the activity areas as you have designed them. Then, walk through the landscape in the way that you envision people moving through it in daily activities. A few factors to think about are:

• Are turf areas easy to access with mowing equipment?
• Are curves open enough to mow without backing and turning?
• Do paths enter and leave an area in a way that does not disrupt its intended use?
• People and animals tend to take the shortest route between two points. Have you designed circulation corridors to respect this tendency?
• Heat pumps, garbage cans, and dog pens can be unpleasant when placed near relaxation areas. Can they be grouped together in an out-of-sight location?

Grade transitions are steps or ramps designed to take you from one level to another. Does your landscape need to be handicapped accessible? If so, this might be one situation where a landscape architect or engineer may be needed to lay out grades. Outdoor steps need to be sturdy, consistent in riser height and tread depth, and highly visible. Outside the house, a riser of six inches or less is recommended and a deep tread, usually eighteen inches, is safe and comfortable.

When choosing materials, it's important to think about their durability, safety, and comfort in an outdoor setting. Stone and brick or concrete pavers are excellent materials for garden construction. They could be wet-laid over a solid foundation with footers a minimum of thirty inches deep. When properly built, they will last a lifetime. Poorly built structures, in contrast, may shift and crack with freezing and thawing. If you are a do-it-yourself type, take the time to find the correct specifications before you begin to tackle such a permanent installation.

For secondary walks and grade transitions, treated or synthetic wood timbers are sometimes used. Be aware that wood steps need to be installed with the same care to avoid shifting and dangerous tripping hazards.

A word of caution about wood is in order. In outdoor settings, it becomes very slippery when damp with dew or rain; in addition, surface water freezes on wood long before surrounding surfaces freeze. If allowed to dry out, wood develops unattractive longitudinal cracks, raised grain, and checkering. Exposure to the elements may cause warping and twisting. Some of these problems can be avoided with professional installation and ongoing maintenance. There are also synthetic wood substitutes on the market that have overcome many of these problems. If you like the look of wood, the synthetics are worth investigating. While they are somewhat more expensive at installation, their long term appearance and functionality is usually worth the added cost.

Hillside properties are not uncommon today. Many builders are developing land that would have been considered undesirable a decade ago. Sloping lots can be quite interesting, but they require special treatment that can significantly increase the cost of landscaping. If you want flat areas for play, furnishings or hobby gardening, a sloping lot will need to be terraced. A level surface is created by cutting into the hillside and placing the excavated soil further down the slope, known as cut and fill or terracing. Terracing a slope requires heavy equipment and usually entails building retaining walls to hold the cut and filled soil in place. This is not a job for most homeowners to do by themselves, and it will add considerably to the cost of landscaping.

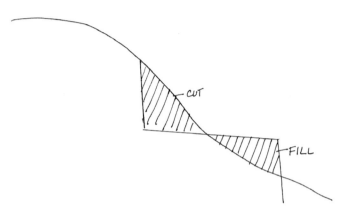

Before any earthwork is undertaken, consider the existing trees on your property. It takes a lifetime or more to grow a mature tree, so if your property came with one or more healthy trees, think of them as a special gift and valuable asset. I recommend designing around them, protecting them, and caring for them. That means keeping construction vehicles off their root zone, which is, at very least, the drip line of the tree. Keep equipment as far away as possible. Smaller trees and shrubs can be transplanted, so carefully evaluate any existing plants and decide what warrants protection. Large plants add value. They significantly improve the appearance of a new landscape, so if you can reuse them, they are usually worth the trouble and expense of having them balled and burlaped by a competent nurseryman, stockpiling and maintaining them, then replanting when construction is completed. Spindly or diseased plants should be discarded.

By now you have probably roughed out the areas for cooking, dining, play, hobbies, and whatever activities you envision for your garden. Now is the time to consider irrigation and lighting. Underground conduits need to be in place before much of the landscaping begins. Those two or three hose bibs in the foundation of the house are woefully inadequate. If your lot is more than a quarter of an acre you will be forced to hook up hoses and drag them around at the risk of damaging valuable plants. It's a great convenience to have frost-proof water hydrants placed at convenient locations throughout the landscape.

Even if lighting is not in your budget at the moment, design it into your plan and have underground conduits placed. Check with your municipality's electrical code before doing anything.

Conduits should go from the nearest electrical connection point, beneath hardscaping, and into areas that will someday hold lighting fixtures. These conduits can be simple PVC pipes or, in the case of pillars, outdoor rated electrical wiring can be incorporated into them at construction, depending on the code in your area. If the infrastructure is in place, an electrician can easily add the electrical connection and lighting fixture when you are ready.

Do you need shade on a sunny terrace? A newly planted tree will take years to provide the desired cover, but an arbor or pergola can provide instant light filtering while adding another dimension to the garden. Supporting posts can be wood, iron, stone, or stucco pillars. A lattice structure will give some immediate shade, and fast growing vines can be added to scramble over the lattice and create a wonderfully cool, leafy room. Depending upon your taste, a pergola can be ornate or simple; either way, it will enhance and extend the appearance of the architecture.

A well-planned garden functions seamlessly to increase your enjoyment of outdoor living. Landscaping is a large investment. With minor renovations and good maintenance practices it should last a lifetime. So take time to plan carefully and research or consult with a competent professional before starting to install your working landscape.

Surface drainage can be managed by diverting it to a dry stream designed to carry water during a heavy downpour. Water can percolate from the surface or it can be collected in a dry well.

This series of terraces facilitates the grade change at the rear of the house while creating an attractive outdoor living and dining room.

Slabs of stone are used to build steps up a long slope. The natural stone complements this informal garden featuring native plantings and overlooking a stream valley and nature preserve.

It is important to think through the electrical and mechanical functions of garden features before construction begins. This natural appearing pond requires both electricity and plumbing hook ups. Pipes and wiring must go in before the liner and permanent structural materials are set in place.

A brick walk intersects the parking court, taking visitors toward the front entrance of the house. An attractive planter further points the way to the front door.

A bluestone terrace is enclosed by low walls that double as informal seating. The smooth surface of the cut stone makes it easy to move furniture, and the expansive size of the area facilitates large outdoor gatherings.

Wood is used for these steps and retaining wall at the end of a driveway. The wall is a neat and relatively inexpensive way of retaining the cut, and the steps lead to a frequently used deck and gardens.

Dappled light enhances the rustic appeal of this mixed material paving. Moss and plantings add to the charm of this small terrace.

Features such as a bench and planters add interest to an entry courtyard.

A fountain creates a dramatic entrance feature. This outdoor room corresponds to the entry foyer inside the door.

An overhead structure diffuses light and creates a vertical connection between the house and garden. Pergolas and arbors add to the sense of enclosure in an outdoor room without obstructing views of the surrounding scenery.

It is very important to think through all the functions of the landscape before construction begins. Interrupting installation with forgotten items can be a costly process, and after construction is completed adding infrastructure becomes very expensive and destructive.

Preserving mature trees gives a sense of permanency to the landscape as well as providing many environmental benefits.

Chapter Three

Designing Garden Space

Mature trees surround this space. Boulders define a small pond that closely resembles a woodland pond. Careful observation allows a designer to duplicate the charm of natural water features.

For many of us, plants are the first things that come to mind when we think of landscaping. However, while plantings are certainly an important and valuable element, they are not the most significant factor in the early stages of garden design. The success or failure of a garden is determined by the effective use of space; in fact, the most successful landscape architects build their reputations on brilliant manipulation of space.

The spaces you create within your landscape will depend on several issues. Of course, the size of your property is a decisive factor. How will you live in your landscape? Do you plan on dining out-of-doors? If so, will you plan intimate family meals or large-scale parties? Do you enjoy growing some of your own food? Does your vision include the serenity of a quiet pond with koi flashing below the surface? Or, do you prefer the drama of a waterfall? Start with a list of how you wish to use the available space. Include all your dreams. You may have to prioritize later, but now is the time for dreaming. Share your wishes with your design professional and be sure they are honored to the extent your budget will allow.

The next step is to start planning. If you are doing your own design, it's much easier and more accurate to start with a survey of your property. If a survey is not available, you can measure the property, as well as the placement of the house, driveway, and other permanent objects, including trees. Draw the plot plan to scale on a sturdy piece of paper, then use tracing paper overlays to work out the details of your landscape. An eight or ten scale (one inch equals eight or ten feet) is fairly easy to work with, allowing enough room to draw details but keeping the plan to a manageable size. Once the plot plan is done, you can start designing the landscape.

With your tracing paper over the base plan, draw circles to designate each desired area. This is called a bubble plan and it is useful, at this stage, for working out the spaces, their sizes, and how they will relate to each other, the house, and other landscape elements. You may use many sheets of tracing paper before you have all the spaces where you want them. This is a very important step in the design process so do not rush it.

When I think of space in the garden, I think in terms of rooms—outdoor rooms that correspond to indoor rooms—and corridors that take you from one to another. The word *place* is a very important one in the lexicon of garden design, and it will be used frequently. It was fully explained in Chapter One (A Sense of Place). Strolling from one point of interest to another is a very enjoyable way of experiencing the garden, more so if those points of interest have a real sense of purpose and place.

Think, for example of an outdoor dining room. A dining area will be most comfortable if it is well defined, with an eye to privacy from the neighbors. A lattice screen, a fence, wall, or interesting plantings at the boundaries could help achieve this goal. There will be a table and chairs for dining al fresco. Their size and style will be determined by the size and type of gatherings you are planning and on your personal sense of style. A fairly smooth surface works best beneath furniture, so you might consider a bluestone or interlocking paver floor. A piece of sculpture or a water feature will further enhance the space and personalize it.

Another possibility is an outdoor kitchen. This can be as simple as a freestanding charcoal grill or as elegant as a stainless steel, state-of-the art cooking facility, complete with refrigeration, hot and cold water, and granite countertops. Herbs, vegetables, and fruits can be grown in containers and beds to enhance the kitchen and keep the freshest possible ingredients close at hand.

Have you ever considered an al fresco exercise room? There are endless interesting possibilities aside from the ubiquitous basketball hoop in the driveway. A bocce ball court, croquet lawn, or horseshoe pit can easily be worked into the landscape. You might enjoy a counter-current swimming pool. This small pool has an adjustable current to allow you to swim for exercise, in much less space than a traditional swimming pool. A putting green or a sport court may be more to your liking. Sport courts come in many sizes and they can be configured for almost any sport. It's a great way to enjoy time with your kids while the whole family gets beneficial exercise.

Many of us enjoy a peaceful spot for relaxing, meditating, or enjoying quiet conversation. A reflecting pool or a quietly burbling fountain add a sense of tranquility to such an area. Benches or chairs—with the emphasis on comfort—encourage lingering and prolong the enjoyment of the colors and fragrances of the garden. Privacy and shade are desirable elements and the serene forms of large leaved hostas and ferns are particularly appropriate in a secluded personal space.

There is even a movement afoot to create outdoor bedrooms, complete with appropriate furnishings. It's not a new idea. Many homes of the Victorian period included sleeping porches. Imagine lying under the stars with crickets singing a lullaby. Outdoor bedrooms aren't for everyone, but, like other outdoor rooms, they have the advantage of drawing you into the world of nature and expanding your awareness of the wonders, large and small, that surround you.

The most functional outdoor spaces are level, with a comfortable surface underfoot. Grades and drainage patterns will be strong factors in determining how you configure your garden. Steep slopes need terracing to become usable space. If you are shopping for a house, it's a good idea to consider the impact of the grades on your desired lifestyle. Hills and valleys can be interesting to look at, but if you want functional activity areas, steep grades will add significantly to the cost of creating your garden. Even if you do not wish to terrace steep slopes, they are difficult and expensive to maintain.

The related issue of drainage is a crucial consideration. High water levels and run-off patterns will complicate landscape planning and construction. It is best to address these issues before you set your heart on a plan. In many municipalities, if a parcel is deemed wetland, it is against the law to disturb or drain it. These naturally occurring wetlands lend themselves to some wonderful gardening opportunities. While many plants require good drainage to thrive, an interesting pallet of moisture loving plants also exists (see rain garden plant list, page 28) In all cases, water, whether from surface runoff or underground sources, needs to be directed away from the house and related structures…a potentially costly process.

Existing natural features such as mature trees, a stream, boulders, or rock outcroppings, can be landscape bonanzas. You cannot grow a tree to substantial size in your lifetime, so if you have one or more in your existing landscape—congratulations! Protect them, cherish them, and design around them. Remember that much of the tree's support system is underground. As noted earlier, roots need to be protected from excavation—even the weight of construction equipment traffic over the root zone will very likely kill a tree.

A stream on your property can be a wonderful landscape asset. It can also be a terribly destructive force—a gentle rivulet can become a raging torrent after several inches of rainfall. You may need professional advice to deal effectively with landscaping your stream so that it continues to be an asset. Environmental protection laws restrict the ways that you may change or disturb a natural streambed. Before undertaking any such changes, check with your state or municipal authorities for permitting requirements.

Boulders can become landscape features, adding character and interest, contrasting with plantings and acting much like a piece of sculpture. Why is it that boulders so often look like asteroids that just landed in the landscape? By observing large rocks in their natural formation, you will learn how to make boulders appear to be naturally occurring features. Notice how they lie in relation to the surrounding terrain and to each other. They are most often partially buried in the ground. Which way does the grain of the stone run? How are plants growing adjacent to, over, or on them?

Boulders are beautiful in their natural surroundings, and the closer you can come to recreating that arrangement, the more attractive and comfortable they will look in the landscape. A rock ledge or outcropping can be worked into the landscape as a seating element, a wall, or steps. It can become a wonderful focal point with plants and lighting. Natural rock configurations can also be turned into waterfalls or stone sculptures. So don't be too quick to dig or blast those rocks out of the way.

When you are planning your landscape, lighting is a must. Lighting can turn your outdoor room into a magical place, carved out of the night. The pool of illumination brings elements into sharp focus against the background of darkness. It creates a cozy, secure space, much like our ancestors must have experienced, as they sat in the light of the campfire. Of course, good path lighting is an important safety feature.

Containers, overflowing with flowering plants and interesting foliage, are wonderful for adding touches of color, texture, and definition to an outdoor room. They are especially valuable in restricted environments—decks, small city gardens, or verandas, for example. You can see how planning a landscape is very much like designing the interior of your home. You make decisions about floors, walls,

furnishings, lighting, and decorative elements, and you may even have a ceiling of overhanging trees or a vine covered arbor.

If you are limited for space, consider combining several uses in one area. Edible plants can be mixed into ornamental beds if you don't have room for a vegetable garden. In the afternoon, the kids can splash in a fountain on the dining terrace. Later in the evening, you entertain friends on the same terrace, with the fountain as a subtle counterpoint to relaxed conversation. A bench in the entry garden can double as a decorative element or a spot for quiet conversation or a moment of meditation. Look around for wasted space, no matter how small, and think how it can be put to use. Can you fit in a vignette of your favorite perennials, a small table and chairs for two, a pebble walk through a shady corridor with a carpet of hostas and ferns? You can make every corner special. That is the nature and the magic of garden design.

After you have designated a space for each desired function, traffic flow and connection with the house needs to be planned. We'll consider these subjects in Chapter Six (Outside and In).

An intimate conversation area is created in an out-of-the-way corner. In every landscape, there are many such spaces. With some thought, they may become the best features in the garden.

Plantings and boulders are used to reinforce the woodland appearance of a city garden edge.

A farmhouse in the south of France inspired this gravel paved entry courtyard with its rustic stone walls, containers, and plantings.

The dining terrace is set apart from the rest of the landscape with walls, a grade change, and plantings.

A serene path in the shade of Redspire Pears. The ground cover is the graceful grass-like, *Hakonechloa macra* 'Aurea'.

A brick terrace is softened by plantings of liriope, nandina, and clematis. While requiring little maintenance, the plantings provide seasonal color and remain attractive through the winter.

A definite sense of place and privacy is imparted by this attractive brick wall. Privacy is further reinforced by the plantings growing above the wall.

Overhead structure and plantings define a dining space in an urban landscape. As they mature, plantings at the property edges will screen neighboring houses from view.

A panel of lawn becomes a special place when surrounded by a graceful seating wall and interesting plantings.

Adjacent to the swimming pool deck, this shaded space offers a retreat from the sunlight and activity while still being a part of the recreation space.

Lattice panels provide privacy, enclosure, and screening of pool equipment—all important functions in this sophisticated urban home landscape.

A large parking court is needed for entertaining at this country property. A low wall creates enclosure without cutting off expansive views.

41

For afternoons of active family fun, this pool and pool house, complete with toilet and shower facilities plus an outdoor kitchen, provide all that is needed to keep dripping bathers from running into the main home.

A grand staircase leads from the upper terrace to the pool and gardens. Plantings help to integrate the strong structural element with its surroundings.

Twin weeping cherries mark the beginning of the formal landscape as visitors arrive on a long driveway to this rural property.

A small pool with fountain and unique sculpture makes this family dining terrace a very interesting and personal space.

A formal garden provides an interesting walk from the rear of the house out to the tree shaded lawns surrounding it.

Mirrored perennial borders create an interesting walkway from the pool and terrace to expansive lawns and gardens in this European inspired landscape.

Chapter Four

Composing the Picture

A formal entryway demonstrates symmetrical balance. The formality is reinforced by the classic form of containers.

In a well-designed landscape, all of the elements work together to create a harmonious and enticing scene. If you are doing your own garden design, or even if you are working with a landscape architect, it is helpful to have a working knowledge of some basic elements of design, such as balance, repetition, line, scale, color, form, and texture.

Each room in your landscape will contain elements specific to its particular function: an outdoor kitchen in one, badminton net in another, and pond with a bench in a third. Just like the rooms in your home, these spaces need to be in harmony with each other. Think how jarring it would be if you decorated your dining room in an Asian motif, your living room in French provincial, and the kitchen in Southwestern style. Similarly, garden rooms that flow into one another need to have a common style or pattern to unify the design. When each room in the garden has a different planting scheme and different hardscape materials, the landscape may start to resemble a series of garden center displays.

Balance is one element of design. It can be either formal or informal. In formal or symmetrical balance, both sides of a centerline are mirror images of each other. In informal or

asymmetrical design, one side may be balanced in height by the other side's spread. Asymmetrical balance may be influenced by volume, texture, and color. Formal or informal, no matter which style suits your taste, balance is an important consideration. When a design is in balance, the individual parts all create a unified whole; the eye flows through the landscape without bouncing from point to point.

Repetition of the same or similar elements and plants throughout the landscape is a unifying technique that holds the composition together and gives continuity to the design. On a large scale property, for example, a combination of evergreen white pine and fast growing Heritage river birch could be used to define areas, screen for privacy, control wind and sun, and frame views. In the first example, the white pines could be repeated throughout the property wherever an evergreen privacy screen, a windbreak, a large evergreen specimen, or a green backdrop is needed. The birches can be repeated where shade, an attractive specimen, and winter interest are desired. Other trees and shrubs can be added to create an interesting and varied landscape, while the pines and birches hold the composition together and give it continuity. The simplicity of this basic scheme allows for imaginative under planting while maintaining integrity of design throughout the landscape. On a smaller property, Korean dogwood and San Jose holly will perform similar functions while growing to a more diminutive scale at maturity.

Elements of consistency throughout a landscape plan indicate a well thought-out concept. This in no way eliminates the addition of contrasting focal points to add drama. In fact, focal points will be much more exciting and apparent when displayed in a harmonious setting. Just as we mentioned earlier in this chapter, garden rooms should mirror interior rooms, in that they should bear some relationship to one another for best effect.

Lines—planned or unplanned—exist in every landscape. The eye naturally follows those lines, and their character will determine one's response to the picture. Some obvious lines are the edges of a paved area, the edge of a bed, the top of a hedge or wall. The tops of trees on an adjacent property can form a line. A formal landscape will often be intersected and defined by straight lines, the informal by sinuous curves. Curving paths that disappear encourage exploration of the garden. Wide straight walks are friendly and welcoming, especially to the handicapped. Smooth horizontal lines are serene and relaxing.

Sight lines can be manipulated to extend the view of the garden, making it appear larger. A line that disappears from view on a neighboring property "borrows" part of that property visually. Lines can be smooth and sinuous or ragged and chaotic. Think of a bed of pachysandra versus a country flower garden. In the first case, your eye follows the consistent green border, while in the second, it bounces from flower to flower. The first is rather restful while the second is energetic. Each of these styles is enjoyable under the right circumstances. It all depends on your taste and the mood you are attempting to establish with your design.

Scale is an interesting concept in the garden. We've all seen a small house sheltered by a large shade tree, which can look nice even though the house and tree are vastly different in scale. We've also seen houses so buried in overgrown shrubbery that they almost disappear—that is unattractive and structurally damaging to the house. As you can see, scale is not an issue for strict rules. New mansions are sometimes surrounded by huge mulch beds dotted with tiny plants—a tribute to optimism or to the enjoyment of the next generation. Garden features need to be scaled to fit the size of the garden and the architecture, but variations in the size of features adds interest. The question to ask yourself is simply: "Does it look right?"

In general, outdoor structures and spaces should be sized larger and stronger than indoor structures. They appear more comfortable and permanent that way. Garden steps should have a deeper tread and lower riser than indoor steps—a tread to riser proportion that would be acceptable indoors may appear daunting or even dangerous in the landscape. Posts, which support an arbor, porch or deck, look more suitable when oversized. Structures appear wobbly with thin supporting members.

The demands of an intended function will also influence the form of landscape features. Beds designed with gently flowing curves make mowing of adjacent lawn easier. Walks should be wide enough to allow two people to walk side by side comfortably. Lighting fixtures need to illuminate walkways and steps for safety. The size and shape of each aspect of your landscape will be influenced by the function it will serve.

Forms help to define style as well. A symmetrically balanced landscape will have a formal appearance. The shapes that reinforce this formality will in themselves be symmetrical—picture the perfect cone shape of a Norway spruce versus the irregular branching pattern of a blue atlas cedar. Reinforce the formal or casual style of your garden by selecting forms that are of similar character. One caution about perfectly balanced plantings—bear in mind that plants may have health problems, weather related damage, or they may even die, leaving your "perfectly balanced" scheme out of balance.

Color influences perception of the landscape in many ways. Bright, bold colors draw attention to themselves. They speak of energy, activity, and excitement. White and soft pastels are more suited to serene, contemplative landscapes. Blues and purples recede. They are best when viewed close-up. Reds, oranges, and yellows come forward in the field of vision. They will stand out at great distances, as does white. What does that tell us about using color in the landscape? Use it with great care. It is a powerful tool—setting mood, drawing attention to or away from a given element.

Texture adds interest to the garden. An all green planting can be fascinating when it includes a variety of textures. Think of broad spreading hostas, delicate sprays of ferns, and the spiky grass-like leaves of Siberian iris. When grouped together, the contrasting forms and textures of these plantings create a charming picture. Large, bold leaves and vines lend a tropical appearance to the garden. Fine textured plants serve as wonderful background for colorful flower borders. A uniform planting of the same texture takes on an architectural appearance, while contrasting textures impart a more natural feeling.

Patterns are closely aligned to texture, although I think of pattern more in regard to the design of light and shadow formed by foliage, or the shape of a particular tree or shrub against a background of light. Patterns are the design of individual leaflets arranged along a fern frond, while texture is the whole of the fern contrasting with surrounding plants.

Alternating light and shadow is a tool of the artist as well as the garden designer. It is used to set a mood, to create interest, contrast, and definition. Sunny areas are energetic and active while shaded enclaves seem quiet, relaxing, restful. Alternating light and shadow through the garden can create a scene that begs to be explored further—drawing you forward to that spot of sun or that shady grove.

Think about the final impression you are trying to achieve when deciding upon matters of texture, color, form, and scale. These and other design concepts enter into every aspect of planning a landscape. They will come up again and again in later discussions of specific garden creations.

Asymmetrical balance creates a casual, unplanned appearance. This landscape balances a springhouse with exuberant plantings—a perfect setting for a structure reminiscent of rural landscapes.

Repetition of similar colors and forms throughout the landscape unifies the design and creates a harmonious experience.

A sweep of perennials creates a line suggesting activity and energy. The assertive flower colors reinforce this feeling.

The smooth flowing lines of the stone wall and adjacent lawn create a picture of peace and serenity, in marked contrast with the busy street behind the evergreen screen.

Large boulders are arranged to serve as a retaining wall and as casual seating around the fire pit. Outdoor structures need to be bold in scale to avoid looking spindly and unsafe.

An entrance walk should be wide enough for two people to walk side by side. A smooth surface insures good footing and is easily cleaned after snowstorms.

Garden steps that are wide and shallow are safe, comfortable, and visually pleasing in an outdoor setting.

The flowing curve of this bed line allows a mower to follow it easily. Maintenance is an important consideration when planning the layout of beds.

In this more formal setting, the beds have also been planned for ease of mowing, with areas of lawn wide enough to accommodate a mower and smooth flowing bed lines.

Warm colors come forward in the field of vision. Red, orange, and bright yellow are happy, active colors that are noticed from a distance.

Even though it is a bold color, purple will recede from view at a distance. Blues and purples are best viewed close up.

The riotous color and texture of this meadow are complementary. Both color and texture add interest to the garden, and both need to be used with care because they make a very definite statement.

Contrasting textures create an exciting picture without relying on color.

Irregular flagstone set in brick creates a crazy quilt pattern that perfectly suits the farmhouse setting where it leads to the kitchen entry.

The elements of design are used to good effect in this well-planned family garden.

Shade and sun alternate to add depth to this enticing scene of plantings and lawn. The bench beckons visitors to come and relax on a summer afternoon.

Chapter Five

The Stylish Garden

A distinctive style complements the architecture of this Pennsylvania farmhouse. Stone walls were a common aspect of the farm landscape in colonial Pennsylvania.

Will it be a woodland retreat, a formal garden, a setting for your sculpture collection, or something completely innovative? Throughout the history of garden design, styles have followed cultural imperatives. The earliest gardens were devoted to producing food and medicinal herbs. Think of the medieval monastery garden, featuring a well at its center and beds of medicinal herbs surrounding it.

In pioneer days, the garden was often the responsibility of the homemaker. She was the cook and caretaker of the family's health, and bore a multitude of other responsibilities as well. With the help of the younger children, she grew much of what the family ate. A no-nonsense garden with beds of vegetables plus medicinal and culinary herbs served her needs. Often the

beds were raised to improve drainage and fenced to keep out hungry animals. Even though they were busy and did not have much in the way of material goods, these pioneer women often found a way to bring some color into their lives by planting a few flowers in the garden. Precious seeds and cuttings were passed from one to another, symbols of friendship and the innate desire for beauty in our lives.

In the Middle East, a scorching climate and the traditions of Islam dictated a garden that included water, flowers, and fruit. Enclosing walls provided safety and seclusion for the women of the household. While sculptural depictions of gods, heroes, and historic figures decorated European gardens, such images were forbidden for the devout Muslim. They turned to geometric forms, colorful tile mosaics, and intricate lattice as decorative elements. So great was the Middle Easterner's love of gardens, that their flowers and forms were woven into carpets, to grace their tents as they traveled across deserts for extended periods of time. As living standards improved throughout the world, gardening shifted from a focus on subsistence to a focus on ornamentation and enjoyment. Extravagant pleasure gardens, landscaped parks, and hunting preserves became outward expressions of wealth and power.

When you visit both public and private gardens in every country of the world, the historic themes are repeated over and over. They speak of some basic drive for order and beauty, common to human beings. Just as language and music arise in fairly predictable order, garden styles follow cultures as they rise and fall throughout the history of mankind. Early garden style was dictated by necessity, climate, cultural imperatives, and the desire to make a statement. Today, our gardens repeat many of the same themes and patterns—sometimes for functional reasons, but often because they are familiar and appealing to us. Fences are employed today for their ornamental qualities as much as for their ability to afford protection from roaming livestock. A profusion of multicolored flowers contained by a picket fence conjures up the image of an English cottage garden. A pea gravel path through plantings of roses, iris, and lavender suggests a garden in the south of France.

A collection of cactus and yuccas emerging from a gravel bed bespeaks a hot, dry climate—perhaps Southern California or New Mexico. When I'm browsing through garden magazines, I have a tendency to skip right over the desert gardens, with their sparse vegetation, stark forms, and unfamiliar textures. I garden in a climate with plentiful rainfall and long winters; it would be a self-defeating struggle to attempt a desert garden here. In a similar vein, I am strongly attracted to gardens I have visited in Mediterranean regions and would love to have olive and lemon trees in mine, but again it would be unrealistic to try to maintain such a garden here in the Mid-Atlantic region. I'm not sure what attracts us to one style more than another. I do know I would be unhappy living with a garden full of cactus and succulents, even though I appreciate their striking form and character. There is a good chance that certain garden styles attract you more than others as well.

In addition to our innate preferences, therefore, we must take into account the climate and culture in which garden styles have evolved. I can develop a garden with a tropical *appearance* in Pennsylvania, but unless I have a heated conservatory, I cannot have a truly tropical garden here. You may want a *Japanese style* garden, but unless you have a staff of gardeners, you probably cannot maintain a true Japanese garden, where every branch is trained for special effect and every falling leaf is quickly removed, except for the one artfully arranged on the mossy path.

An important consideration when discussing style is the architecture to which the garden will relate. A garden that is very different in style from your house can be visually unsettling. Using the previous examples, a tropical appearing garden

would not be a good fit for my Pennsylvania farmhouse and the stark simplicity of a Japanese garden would seem strange surrounding an ornate Victorian house. Picture a Georgian colonial in a desert garden. Some styles just don't complement each other. Chances are, however, if you choose to live in a Georgian colonial, your tastes run toward a landscape design that will suit it.

There are no strict rules when it comes to style. It is a combination of taste and necessity. If you have always admired Japanese gardens, for example, study them carefully. What is it that attracts you? Is it the serenity? Is it the way in which water is used, the discipline and restraint of the design? Or is it features such as stone basins and lanterns? Could you incorporate some of those elements into your landscape, and feel a sense of satisfaction? Or do you need to hire a Japanese landscape architect and craftsmen to create an authentic Japanese garden including a teahouse in which to entertain your friends?

There is much discussion among landscape designers concerning regionally appropriate styles. Part of that conversation concerns the use of native plants versus exotics and part of it centers on establishing a recognizable "sense of place." Is a Mediterranean inspired garden appropriate in Pennsylvania? Should a contemporary home in Delaware be framed by a tropical appearing garden? Some designers feel we should design our home landscapes to mimic the natural environment in our region of the country. Others refer to characteristics of historic landscapes for their inspiration.

Shortly after we bought the property where we now live, we removed a swimming pool and its surrounding decking. In its place, I have developed a meadow—much like the meadows where I often played as a child in central Pennsylvania. The basic planting is native grasses, many from seeds I collected on walks with our dogs. Native plants such as butterfly weed, perennial sunflower, spiderwort, *asters*, and meadow *lobelia* paint a bright palette against the graceful grasses. I have added hybrids and exotic plants for their flower color, but I've chosen those with "meadowy" forms. We mowed paths through the tall grasses and placed two Adirondack chairs at the back of the meadow. This garden, alive with birds, brings us endless pleasure as it constantly changes throughout the season. It embodies "a sense of place" for me and it's a magical bag of tricks for the many visitors to our garden.

A new style of garden design has recently emerged, one based on the way that plant communities occur naturally. Designers and horticulturists such as Noel Kingsbury, Piet Oudolf, Ken Druse, and Rick Darke have produced beautifully illustrated books on the subject. This style boasts exuberant plantings full of color and texture with minimal maintenance. It can look untidy at times, and it will not appeal to everyone. If you find this concept attractive, the work of the authors cited above is an excellent resource for developing your own natural garden.

Do your ecological concerns dictate a palette of native plants, or do you prefer to use plants that have been developed for showy flowers, disease resistance, or compact growth? Are you drawn to formal clipped hedges, boxwood parterres, or pattern bedding? In the end, only you can answer the questions posed by the multitude of possibilities. The best advice I can give on the matter is to observe carefully what others have done. Look at the landscapes of houses you visit and drive past. Stroll through public gardens. Browse the pages of this book. Books and magazines are a treasure trove of ideas. Some styles of landscaping will sing out to you, some you will find unattractive, and others will quickly fade from your memory. There is an instinctive attraction to the style that is right for you. When you experience such an attraction, make note of it. Pay attention to the elements that make it pleasing to you. Careful observation will allow you to choose a landscape style that brings pleasure for many years.

A bee skep and potted herbs, informally arranged, are appropriate accents to this reproduction colonial farmhouse and garden.

A bed of easy-care rudbeckia fit perfectly in this country garden scene. A rustic stone springhouse in the background could house pool equipment or garden tools, as it further reinforces the farmhouse theme.

Symmetrical forms and balanced plantings establish the formality of a garden surrounding this stately house.

The impressive entry to this expansive property is reminiscent of imposing manor houses from an earlier century. A well thought-out and consistent style gives a garden its character.

This potager or ornamental vegetable garden is modeled on a medieval monastery garden. The sculpture at the center takes the place of the well, with the garden divided into quadrants by walkways.

Lines of a contemporary house are softened by matching columns supporting a shade arbor. The arbor shelters sitting areas from the intense sun while creating a relaxed country style in keeping with the homeowner's lifestyle.

The well-defined style of this garden clearly demonstrates the designer's intent to unify landscape and house. A strong theme such as this keeps the garden from becoming just a collection of plants and structures.

Lush plantings, a stone wall, and the lantern are all traditional landscape elements of the Mid-Atlantic states. A landscape such as this is at home with the climate and cultural heritage of this region.

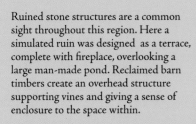

Ruined stone structures are a common sight throughout this region. Here a simulated ruin was designed as a terrace, complete with fireplace, overlooking a large man-made pond. Reclaimed barn timbers create an overhead structure supporting vines and giving a sense of enclosure to the space within.

A controlled woodland garden is a relaxing contrast to the city street on which this home is located.

65

This native plant meadow thrives, with moderate maintenance, in the climate and soils to which it adapted. Native plants can be used in more structured designs as well. Most will have a tendency to spread and grow exuberantly in a garden setting.

In this garden, native grasses and cultivated plants join forces to create a seasonally interesting scene with moderate maintenance requirements. An unstructured style such as this does not suit every style of architecture and personal taste.

An exuberant style of garden is gaining popularity. Known as the *"New American Garden,"* it is inspired by natural plant communities. This style has its roots in the lush perennial gardens of the Netherlands and England, as well as the prairies of the mid-west.

In stark contrast with the "New American Garden," this stately home is accented by the restrained formality of a clipped hedge. Hedges such as this can be costly in term of time and labor.

A welcoming courtyard, enclosed by stone walls, reinforces the Mediterranean style of this home's architecture.

This simple entry garden bids a warm welcome with a bench, colorful flowers, and a comfortably wide path.

A lovely iron gate between stone pillars leads to a pool and terraces interspersed with plantings and surrounded by lawns.

This collection of garden features makes a statement regarding the homeowner's personal style. While this may or may not be your style, the most interesting gardens bear the stamp of their creators.

Chapter Six

Outside and In

Ahhhh! Home at last! Whether coming home from work, from an extended trip, or simply from the mall, you should enjoy an "ahhhh" moment when you arrive at your front door. In addition to bringing joy to your heart, your entry landscape expresses your unique style and personality. It can be a welcoming and memorable experience for your guests too—a sort of preview of your good taste and hospitality.

An entrance garden makes a statement to the world, in the same way that the architecture and furnishings of your home make a statement about your lifestyle and preferences. It welcomes you and your family and it makes a first impression when guests arrive. It is especially important for this garden to be attractive in every season. After all, this is the most public area of your home.

What are the essential elements of the entrance garden? A convenient, safe, and accessible walkway, obvious convergence on the front door, and adequate lighting all come to mind. Walk surfaces can be stone or brick pavement, pea gravel, or concrete, either poured or installed as pre-cast pavers. Each of these materials will lend a certain character to the walkway. Within these categories there are many choices of color, style, and texture that allow you to make the statement you wish.

A smooth, cut bluestone walk for instance, creates a clean, uniform image that works with either contemporary or traditional architecture. On the other hand, the rustic appeal of natural, uncut brownstone paving is better suited to an informal or country style home. Pea gravel, an excellent choice for light traffic areas, imparts a distinctly European look and a subtle

An unusual pavement pattern in flagstone and Belgian block leads through colorful beds of annuals and flowering shrubs to the front door.

crunch underfoot. It is also better suited to the casual landscape. Concrete pavers come in ever-increasing choices of styles and colors. Especially attractive are some of the newer tumbled pavers and those with irregularities suggesting a natural material.

Have you ever stood in front of a house wondering which door to enter? Why make it hard for your friends to find their way? The front door should be the focal point of your entrance garden—put that door in the spotlight! And speaking of spotlights, the front of your house can look beautiful in the soft glow of well-designed landscape lighting. Lighting accents the architecture and plantings as well as illuminating the walkway to create a safe and reassuring trip from the parking area to the front door.

By closely integrating your house and garden, you extend the usefulness of both. To begin with, you can use landscape elements to frame the best features of your house, and to hide its less pleasing aspects. Almost every house has one view that is less than lovely. Whether that view includes the pool equipment, a fuel tank, the heat pump, or the electric meter, it is not designed to be a visual enhancement. Such functional elements need to be accessible for servicing, but do you want to look at them?

A low fence or lattice screen is often the best choice for screening these utilities. The meter reader or the person who fills the tank may not hold your plants in high regard, and you risk ending up with plant breakage, wear and tear, or dieback from the toxic effects of fuel spillage. Plants may overgrow heat pumps or air conditioning compressor units, cutting down on needed airflow. This can reduce efficiency or even contribute to the unit burning out. At the same time, heated air blowing over vegetation may cause burning of leaves and dieback.

Are you moving into new construction? One reason new developments look raw and…well…naked, is that the houses are standing out there all alone with only those poor, skinny little trees as companions. What those neighborhoods need is big trees to soften their harsh geometry and tie them to the surrounding landscape. I have driven through neighborhoods of very modest houses surrounded by mature trees and thought, "That looks like a nice place to live." When I move to a new home, the first things I invested in are the largest trees I can afford. It doesn't take a lot of trees if they are carefully placed for the best effect.

Trees serve many purposes. They shade the house or terrace from the sun, act as a windbreak, frame the structure, add seasonal interest, and provide leaves for compost. What a bargain! They grow large…larger than most of us can imagine when we look at them in the nursery. A large shade tree (such as maple, oak, or linden) planted at eight to ten feet will grow to twenty feet in seven to ten years. Some trees grow even faster. Keep in mind that all trees are not equal in terms of value, longevity, maintenance requirements, and seasonal interest. It is worth taking the time to research a tree species before you consider installing it.

Fast growing trees are sometimes short-lived. Others, such as American beech, are so slow growing that they may not pro-

vide the needed shade or desired framing in your lifetime. Some have insect or disease problems and some trees, such as the sweet gum, drop litter constantly. Be especially cautious about fruit bearing trees near paved areas. Fruit, such as dogwood berries or crabapples, may be attractive on the tree, but on the terrace or driveway it can produce a sticky, hard-to-clean mess that attracts bees and other insects.

In our area, I often see young spruce or blue atlas cedars planted right up next to the house, near the front door. My guess is that they are intended as accent plants, to draw attention to the entrance. However, both of these evergreens are wonderful, long-lived, ornamental specimens that grow to thirty feet high and nearly as wide. In a few years, the homeowner will be left with the choice of destroying a beautiful tree or attempting to move it away from the door. Sadly, the tree always loses. It is almost impossible to dig a root ball on a large tree growing close to the house, without risking damage to the house and/or walks leading to the door.

So, place trees carefully. Even those listed as dwarf or compact will grow much larger than you can imagine. For example, a dwarf Alberta spruce matures at ten to twelve feet in height

No less colorful and welcoming is this secondary entrance, with an arbor drawing attention to the convenient door.

71

and four to six feet wide at the base. Is that what you had in mind when you planted a "dwarf"? Give plants room to develop their beautiful, natural form without the need to whack them into distorted shapes or to remove them when they reach their peak value as landscape specimens. And get to know the tree you are choosing. Do the research. If you don't have time, do go to an established garden center (not a discount chain) and talk to a knowledgeable nurseryman.

Be sure to include the sizzle and splash. There's nothing like a fire pit to gather the family together at dusk. A well-designed fire pit is a great attraction for people of all ages. Our designers surround them with large boulders to provide permanent seating and to reflect the heat. A fire pit extends your garden pleasures into cool weather. It is a real magnet to attract your kids—even the teenagers—to spend an evening around the fire. You will find that conversation flows naturally in the warm glow…perhaps a legacy from our forebears sharing tales and adventures around the campfire. An outdoor fireplace will produce similar results.

Water features provide the splash. They are available in so many forms and price ranges that I would go so far as to say no garden should be without one. Water is a very special element, adding excitement and interest in every season. Yes, ponds do take some maintenance, but with the newer systems, a knowledgeable designer can create a pond that is very nearly maintenance free. Waterfalls are another great addition if well executed. Ponds, artificial streams, and waterfalls are best left to professional installation. Before signing a contract with any company, be sure to see some examples of work they have done. I have unfortunately seen many that were executed by inexperienced or unobservant installers and that resemble the aftermath of an earthquake, with rocks piled at odd angles and unlikely positions.

Fountains create very compelling focal points. Many can simply be set up, filled with water, and plugged in. Depending on their size and mechanical capacity, fountains produce anything from a cheery burble to a loud patter. The splashier ones are good for screening noise from neighbors or nearby traffic. Wall fountains are a classic touch and create an attractive focal point for blank wall space. A sturdy hanger, an electric outlet, and a few gallons of water are all that is needed to bring a wall fountain to life…and bring life to your garden.

Be aware that water in a garden will attract birds, frogs, and all manner of wildlife. This can be a positive or a negative, depending upon your point of view. As with any garden feature, think it over carefully and consider every aspect before committing.

So, we have addressed the entry, the framing and screening, the access, and the sizzle and splash. What else is important when fitting the garden to the house? Traffic flow is an important consideration. How will your family enter and leave the house? What is the shortest route between the back door and the sports court? When you plan outdoor rooms, think through their uses. What will you need to carry to that room and how often will you need to carry it? Taking furniture inside for winter storage is not as much of a priority as reaching the dining table from the kitchen for daily meals. For those who enjoy dining al

fresco, the trip can become arduous if the distance is great or obstacles such as stairs must be negotiated.

Some designers advocate letting the traffic flow design itself by initially not doing anything. After a period of time, you simply place the walkways where paths have been worn. Meanwhile, of course, mud is being tracked onto the carpeting, and no one is happy about that. I believe that thoughtful planning can establish practical circulation patterns and reinforce them.

To begin the process, lay out your active and passive use areas on paper and draw lines between them. Sit and think, "If I were little Buster and I wanted to go from the garage (where the basketball is kept) to the sports court, which route would I take?" It is fairly simple to figure most of this out. It becomes more challenging, however, when an outdoor room, perhaps a sitting area you have your heart set on, is located at the junction of several direct routes. Traffic could turn the space into a corridor instead of a peaceful conversation or relaxation area. That is when you plan an alternate route and do some judicious planting to redirect traffic. It can be done—there are plants that have been used to keep bulls confined. You may not want them in your landscape, but people, like water, tend to take the path of least resistance and you can find plants to create that resistance.

You will want primary walkways. Those will be at least wide enough for two people to walk side by side. In constant use, they should be paved with a material that will withstand traffic, remain attractive, and provide even walking surface. They also need to be designed to drain quickly after a storm. Secondary walkways—the route to the garage personnel door for example—may be narrower, but still smooth, sturdy, and well constructed. Garden paths can be surfaced with uncut paving stones, brick, or a combination of materials. A loose aggregate, such as pea gravel, is often used in this setting. Finally, plan for the narrow paths that seek out hidden places in the landscape. They can be marked out with rough stepping stones set in the lawn, or a mulch of shredded bark or wood or a loose aggregate. These intriguing paths disappear around a bend and beckon to the adventurous soul. They may lead to a hidden fort, a tree house, a secret garden, or a frog pond.

The last, but certainly not the least, important consideration in planning involves the view from your windows. Rooms where you will sit or stand for periods of time deserve a wonderful view with changing seasonal interest. Walk through the house and take note of windows where the view is important, then plan accordingly. For example, I designed a planting bed near the center of our bluestone paved dining terrace, to create a pleasant view from the French doors of the dining room. In addition to the view, the bed serves to establish traffic flow and activity areas within the terrace. It's important to look at your garden from both inside and out and to think of the house and garden as a unit—one big living area with the exterior extending the interior spaces and surrounding you with lovely views, privacy, and the pleasures of changing seasons. In my planting plan, I also include cut flowers and materials to bring in and decorate my indoor rooms—just one more way of joining the house and garden.

A flowering tree and bulb plantings welcome spring as well as guests. Comfortable and highly visible steps lead to an elevated entranceway.

A formal entrance is accented by sophisticated plantings and graceful iron railings.

A secondary entrance at the same house is embellished with planters and a bench. The trellis adds interest to an otherwise plain expanse of wall.

An enclosing wall defines an outdoor dining room, with a graceful urn as elegant accent piece.

Steps lead directly from the parking area to a deck and terrace used for frequent outdoor entertaining.

Breakfast on the terrace is always a pleasure at this intimate table for two. Plantings screen the space from view and create a cool green oasis.

An attractive pool house provides all the amenities for elegant entertaining. It also houses pool and garden equipment out of sight.

An enclosure of fence screens heat pumps from view, without blocking air flow to the units. The fence is in character with the house and matches other fencing on the property.

A wide lawn path leads through a perennial garden between the pool and lawn. The fence enclosing the pool extends beyond this garden to divide garden rooms from the sweeping lawns surrounding them.

A dramatic entrance introduces visitors to an elegant country estate.

While a stone path leads off to a secondary door, the generous proportions of the brick walk leave no doubt as to which is the main entrance.

A man-made water feature closely resembles a natural stream and pond. The balance of plantings and open water keeps the pond clean and its inhabitants healthy.

A steep slope was terraced with stone walls to create lawn areas and paved outdoor rooms for entertaining. The remaining slope was planted with native perennials and day lilies for ease of maintenance.

Sculpture and containers personalize this cozy sitting area. It is one of a series of outdoor rooms that flow into each other and to the house.

Another area in the same garden provides space for large parties. Plantings frame views of the pool and the peaceful countryside.

An arbor is designed to shade and enclose a dining area in an urban neighborhood. Plantings at the periphery of the one-third acre property provide screening from neighboring houses.

A small island divides traffic headed to the service area from guest parking at the front of this residence.

A generous parking court is defined by bands of interlocking pavers. The pavers will withstand traffic as they soften the expanse of blacktop near the entrance to the house.

When designing, views from the windows are important considerations. It is also important to keep large plants far from windows and doors so they do not interfere with light and access as they mature.

Chapter Seven

Maintenance by Design

Trees, lawn, and hardy shrubbery combine to create an inviting garden with relatively low maintenance.

Mowing, weeding, mulching, pruning, fertilization…how much of it do you want to do? What are you physically capable of doing and how much can you afford to have done by others? Garden maintenance is another item on the growing list of considerations when designing your landscape. If gardening is your hobby, you may be very happy spending some weekends working among your plantings. If you have no interest in doing the work yourself, can you afford to hire a landscape maintenance firm to do it for you?

Trees

Imagine a pyramid of landscape maintenance activities, ranking them as to time and effort required. At the peak of the pyramid (meaning it requires the least time and effort) is tree maintenance. Trees need some attention when they are young—watering during periods of drought, corrective pruning, insect control. As they mature, a check-up by a qualified arborist every two to three years should be all that is needed to keep them healthy and strong.

Trees make a valuable contribution to your landscape when they drop their foliage. Fallen leaves may be a chore to collect, but don't dispose of them. They are a great source of humus—the best product for improving soil texture, moisture holding capacity, and plant health—and they're free. Simply pile them in an out-of-the-way place and let them break down over winter, then use them to mulch beds or work into the soil when preparing to plant.

A perennial border such as this requires considerable time and effort. To keep such a border healthy and neat, perennials must be weeded frequently, dead headed, cut back after blooming, and divided regularly. The payoff is colorful flowers and year round textural interest.

Be sure your trees are planted high enough so that the root flare is above the soil surface. Keep the area over the root zone free of competing plant material such as weeds, lawn, or ground covers. Throughout their life, protect your trees from exuberant string trimmers, which leave ugly scars and weaken them by opening the bark to insects and disease. Trees benefit from a wide ring of mulch, no more than two to three inches deep, over the root zone. Too much mulch weakens the root system and will lead to serious damage. Mulch should not be piled against the trunk—in fact it should not be touching the bark of the tree at all. It always saddens me to see trees with a volcano shaped mound of mulch clasping their trunk, because I know they are destined for trouble and a shortened lifespan.

Lawns

Next on the pyramid of landscape maintenance I would place lawn maintenance. The biggest chore in lawn maintenance is weekly mowing throughout the growing season. Grass will often go dormant during the heat and dryness of summer in our Mid-Atlantic states. If you don't water the lawn, it will give you a respite from mowing in the warmest weather. It also avoids some of the turf fungus problems that spring up in the heat of summer, especially on irrigated turf. This dormant period is a normal, healthy state of self-preservation. However, if the sight of browned out turf causes you distress, you can add an irrigation system to your lawn.

An automatic irrigation system should run every four to eight days. It needs to run long enough so the water penetrates three to six inches into the soil. Daily, shallow watering weakens grass, encourages weed growth, and wastes water. Powdery mildew and other fungal diseases thrive on over-watered lawns in hot weather. If the system is not designed and directed properly, run-off or overspray from irrigation may harm or kill trees, shrubbery, perennials, and ground covers. Irrigate or not—you need to be aware of both sides of the equation when you make that decision.

We have been sold the idea that grass needs to be treated and fertilized, watered, and attended to more or less constantly. Not true! To discourage weeds and maintain health, the lawn should be mowed no shorter than three inches, with one-half inch clipped off at each mowing. Keep the mower blades sharp and leave the clippings on the lawn. That half inch of clippings is barely noticeable and it will add fertility and humus to the soil. Every other year or two send a soil sample off to be tested by your local extension service or university soils lab. They will provide recommendations for fertilization and PH adjustment to keep your lawn healthy and green. You may be surprised at how little it takes.

Meadows have been touted as low maintenance alternatives to lawns. I love the appearance of a well-tended meadow, but I have extensive experience with their maintenance. Those fields of bright wildflowers in the catalogues and calendars would have you believe that a meadow is a thing of beauty, requiring little effort. Don't believe it. Unless you can turn your back on "weeds," a meadow is a maintenance nightmare. Native grasses are agonizingly slow to germinate, while clover, dandelion, vetch, and thistle will happily take over the meadow.

When a meadow is finally established, it requires constant monitoring and weed control. Poison ivy, multiflora rose, Japanese honeysuckle, ragweed and mare's tail seem to appear over night. Seedling trees grow up faster than you ever thought possible. In nature, a meadow is a disturbed area on its way to becoming a forest, and you will find your meadow quickly moving toward that goal unless, armed with Round-up, shovel, and a strong back, you intercede. An annual burn-off is a good solution to reducing meadow maintenance, but many municipalities do not allow burning. If you have your heart set on a meadow, it is best to find a meadow consultant with a good reputation to guide you through installation and maintenance.

Shrub Beds

Next in the pyramid of maintenance requirements are shrub beds. Shrubs should be grouped in beds both from a design standpoint and to reduce maintenance and keep them healthy. They should not be spotted here and there on the lawn. If properly spaced and maintained, shrub beds will fill in and cover the soil, discouraging most weeds from sprouting beneath them. Established shrub beds rarely need fertilization. If you have chosen appropriate shrubs for your moisture and climate conditions, insects and diseases are not likely to be a problem.

A two-inch layer of mulch, applied to shrub beds annually, will maintain soil texture and further discourage weed growth. The mulch can be shredded *bark* or *root mulch* that you purchase, a mixture of leaves and grass clippings, your homemade compost, or a combination of any of these. The popular dyed mulches on the market today are shredded waste wood such as old pallets or construction waste. They rob plants of nutrients as they break down and they may harbor termites. To me, their artificial colors appear harsh and unattractive in the landscape. Be sure you are getting bark or root mulch when you buy.

Flower Gardens

I love my flower gardens. They are lush—overflowing with blossoms from early spring until late fall. I spend many, many hours weeding, feeding, staking, cutting back, deadheading, mulching, dividing, watering, and watching over them. For me it is a labor of love. However, there are possibilities for growing flowers that require much less work. You could have a simple cut flower garden where flowers are grown and maintained much like a vegetable garden. You can even put a row or two of flowers in the vegetable garden to be maintained along with the crops. You can tuck a few bulbs, annuals, or perennials in front of shrubs for a touch of relatively carefree color.

Perennial borders come in many styles. A few are discussed in Chapter Eight (Planting Plans). In the traditional cottage garden, most of the landscape consists of perennials and flowering shrubs. Another traditional flower garden features the formal border, often grown in front of an evergreen hedge to provide a background for the colorful blooms. There is an exciting world-wide movement toward creating exuberant, carefree perennial gardens by intermixing grasses and perennials. In these schemes, robust plants are closely spaced to crowd out weeds and fading flowers are allowed to remain on the plants, producing attractive seed heads and eliminating the chore of cutting back. Although this is sometimes referred to as "The New American Garden," the roots of this movement are international.

These new perennial gardens work with nature and their mix of textures and colors resemble naturally occurring combinations of plants. To succeed, this style of design demands knowledge of cultural requirements so that plants and grasses can be carefully matched to the existing environment. To learn more about these gardens, see James van Sweden's *Bold Romantic Gardens* or Noel Kingsbury's *The New Perennial Garden*.

As a rule of thumb, flower gardens are at the bottom of the maintenance pyramid, meaning they will require a significant commitment in time and energy to keep them growing and looking well. When designing flowers into your landscape, the main consideration should be the level of maintenance you are willing to provide. There are high maintenance and low maintenance flowers. In the Appendix, I have compiled a list of reliable, robust, and low maintenance plants to get you started.

Every plant—tree, perennial, shrub, lawn, or ground cover—has its preferred growing conditions. If you locate a sun loving plant in deep shade it will be weak, spindly, and disease prone, and most likely will not flower. By the same token, a shade loving plant will suffer from sunburn and dryness and be prone to insect damage if planted in full sun. An example from my own experience is the story of my *Pieris japonica*. In my landscape, I have two *P. japonica* 'Dorothy Wyckoff'. One is planted in light shade and the other receives full afternoon sun. The one growing in light shade is lovely—covered with glossy dark green foliage year around and pale pink blossoms in earliest spring. The Pieris in the sun has to be treated several times a year for lacebug and spider mite infestations, looks yellow and unhealthy from the insect predation, and is two-thirds the size of the shrub growing in its preferred condition. In its native habitat, Pieris occurs as an understory plant, growing in the shade of mature trees. That is the condition under which it thrives.

To save a good deal of money and growing time, do your research before selecting plants. Growers tag their plants with some information to guide your choices. They will tell you if the plant enjoys dry, well-drained soil or will tolerate moisture, as well as whether to plant it in sun or shade. Some plants need to be sheltered from the wind, others can withstand its buffeting. No matter what your site conditions, you can find plants that will thrive. For a healthy, attractive garden, do the research and buy plants that desire the conditions present in your garden. It's worth taking the time to look up horticultural requirements, rather than enduring the disappointment of plant failures and replacements.

Container plantings may be used to add pizzazz to the garden without significantly increasing maintenance chores,

much like spices add interest to a meal without adding calories. Containers have become very popular in recent years, as they are great fun to design and add wonderful splashes of color and texture just where you need them. If you choose frost-proof containers, they will enhance the quiet beauty of your winter garden as well.

It's fun to change container plantings throughout the growing season. For a summer display, you can select from a wealth of annuals and foliage plants—even shrubbery, ornamental grasses, and perennials for large containers. Be sure to wait until after May 15 (usually our latest frost date) before planting out tender annuals or plants that have been grown in a greenhouse. Container gardens do need regular watering—daily in the hottest weather—and fertilization. I use a slow release fertilizer that needs to be applied only once or twice during the growing season.

Some people enjoy growing vegetable and herb plants in containers. These can be placed close to the kitchen door for convenience, and vegetables combined with flowers create some wonderful effects. When the summer container garden begins to look weary, substitute fall flowering plants or pansies. Pansies survive and grow roots over winter, so they're ready to put on a brilliant display in spring. While bulbs will freeze over winter if planted directly into the container and left outdoors, pot-grown tulips and daffodils can be added in the spring.

Small evergreens from pots are often planted in containers for winter interest. However, since their roots are not protected as they would be in the garden, they frequently die from the intense freezing and thawing that takes place above ground. As an alternative, I often tuck some branches of winterberry and needled evergreens among my pansies to add color for the winter months.

I could write a whole chapter on pruning, but many others have written comprehensive books on the subject. I suggest obtaining a reference volume, such as Lewis Hill's *Pruning Made Easy: A Gardener's Visual Guide to When and How to Prune Everything, from Flowers to Trees*. This is important. Thousands of dollars worth of valuable plants are destroyed each year by poor pruning technique. Even if you are hiring a contractor to do the work, you will need to evaluate their technique and provide direction. Many companies hire inexperienced people every spring and send them out with minimal training. If you decide to do your own pruning, throw away the hedge shears and keep your pruning tools clean and sharp.

Many homeowners prefer hiring a maintenance company to assist with garden chores. It takes some research, however, to find the right contractor. A great deal of damage can be done to your valuable landscape by untrained technicians. When you are interviewing prospective contractors, request a list of current customers and take the time to check with them, asking in-depth questions. Price is not the only consideration. Ask contractors about their training program, both the technical and safety aspects. Also inquire whether the same crew and foreman will be doing your work each week. If new people show up each time, your preferences and instructions may be lost; and do you really want people you have never seen before working around your house?

I recommend using a service that posts the company name and phone number prominently on their trucks and whose crews are dressed in identifiable uniforms. Be sure the contractor is licensed and insured. I use a company that treats its employees well and has little turnover. I don't want to entrust a brow beaten, disgruntled person with my valuable landscaping. This company's crews are well equipped with good tools and safety equipment and their supervisors are courteous and co-operative. They always take a few minutes to check in with me to see if I'm satisfied. I feel it's an indication of a well-managed and reliable company and their service has supported this impression.

While plants take the most frequent maintenance, other landscape elements need care, as well. Concrete or wood decking needs to be sealed annually to remain attractive and durable. Outdoor wood looks best if stained or painted. When left to weather naturally, it will crack and check. Consider using a composite wood for a more carefree option to natural wood. Natural wood dries, causing longitudinal cracking and raised grain with the possibility of splintering.

Stone or brick, set in mortar over a concrete pad, will need to have occasional moss and algae removal if located in a shaded area. The growth of this moss and algae will create a "slip and fall" hazard if not eliminated. Joints will eventually need to be repointed as the mortar cracks and crumbles. Dry laid installations will require weed control in the sand filled joints. A granular, pre-emergence herbicide, swept into the joints in early spring and later in the summer, will greatly reduce the weeding chores.

Landscape maintenance is an important consideration to be addressed when you are designing. Think through your lifestyle. How much time can you realistically allocate to landscape maintenance and how much can you afford to have done by a contractor? Think also about how much you enjoy the manual labor involved and design appropriately—but be aware that *every* landscape will need some level of maintenance.

This comfortable outdoor room requires very little maintenance to remain attractive year round.

Shade and lush ground covers make weed control an easier task. Hostas are an excellent choice for the shade garden. Their broad leaves and dense growth crowd out unwanted volunteers.

A wood deck such as this one needs to be sealed to maintain its beauty and integrity. Composite woods have become pleasing substitutes for wood and they require less maintenance.

A combination of trees, shrubbery, and perennials adds seasonal color with limited maintenance. Perennials run the gamut from those that require considerable care to those that grow like "weeds" and are robust enough to crowd out unwanted ones.

These small terraced beds are easy to maintain. They break up an expanse of paving and ease a grade change attractively.

No weeds allowed! Liriope is a very effective ground cover. Its billowing texture and dark green color are added benefits to an attractive garden workhorse.

Dry laid stone paving is casual and attractive in appearance. However, weeds will find their way into the joints between stones. They are best controlled with contact and pre-emergence herbicides.

A mixed perennial border such as this will require weekly maintenance throughout the growing season.

This closely planted border of daylilies, sedum Autumn Joy and Fountain Grass is under planted with daffodils. There are flowers blooming from early spring to fall and the bed requires very little maintenance. The robust perennials cover fading bulb foliage and crown out most weeds.

Daylilies are one of the lowest maintenance perennials. They make an excellent groundcover with their dense foliage and large flowers, freely produced throughout the summer. They are adaptable to a wide variety of soil and light conditions as well.

A pea gravel terrace requires little maintenance. A bit of weed control and an occasional raking are all that is required. The combination planting adds color and privacy and also requires little maintenance.

An espalier, such as this, is a distinctive feature, but it will need frequent pruning to maintain its attractive pattern. This can be a satisfying project for a dedicated hobby gardener—or a source of frustration for most of us.

Even vegetables can be low maintenance when grown in dense blocks such as this lettuce. The frame can support a cover to extend the season of harvest in the fall and allow early planting in spring.

Container gardens add splashes of color anywhere they are needed. They will require daily watering and monthly feeding during the growing season.

Chapter Eight
The Planting Plan

At last we have arrived at the design of the finishing touches—the planting plan. After all the hard work of thinking through the functional areas, planning hardscaping, and laying out infrastructure, this should be fun. Plants are innately attractive to most of us. They add life to the new landscape. The downside is that they can become a maintenance nightmare if not used wisely.

In the Appendix, I feature a selection of plants chosen for their beauty, ease of maintenance, and reliability. But first, just for a moment, we need to think of plants not as plants, but as forms, volume, and functional elements. With an overlay on your plan, draw in simple outlines to indicate where you need screening, shade, a focal point to draw attention, a decorative element, or traffic direction. Note areas where you wish to reduce maintenance—on a steep slope for example. These are some of the ways plantings will function in your landscape.

Plants can be used in a highly structured way, acting much like walls. The

Plants are some of the most rewarding features of a well designed landscape.

strong line of a clipped hedge resembles the geometry of city streets and buildings. While very appealing to some, this use of plants requires a high level of maintenance. An informal sense of enclosing walls can be achieved with unclipped shrubs or evergreens. Fine texture plants work well in both of these schemes. A great favorite of mine is *Buxus sempervirens* or American boxwood. A rich dark green year around, this plant responds well to heavy pruning or grows into lovely billowing mounds if left to develop naturally. *Buxus microphylla koreana*, the Korean boxwood, is a good choice if you need smaller scale. A more casual enclosure can be achieved with a mixed planting of evergreen and deciduous shrubs.

Shrubbery is used for screening and defining space and adding seasonal interest. Some shrubs are spectacularly colorful in bloom and foliage color, some violently so. I stay away from the most flamboyant ones since they tend to draw too much attention to themselves and "punch holes" in the landscape design. Some may enjoy the bold scarlet of burning bush in the fall or

Kurume azalea in spring, but they are too flashy for me. It is a matter of personal taste. Don't overlook berry-bearing shrubs. *Viburnum*, beauty berry, and hollies can add months of color to a planting scheme.

Another way in which plants can function is by reducing maintenance of difficult areas such as slopes. Ground covers do a good job of out-competing weeds in shaded areas. Remember, a ground cover doesn't need to be a low growing plant. In fact, taller plants are even more effective at keeping out competing weeds. Some of the most effective ground covers are the shade loving hostas, pachysandra, certain ferns, liriope, and many perennials such as *Begonia grandis*, the hardy begonia. Full sun makes weed control more difficult, but it can still be achieved with sweeps of robust growers such as *Hemerocallis*, *Rudbeckia*, or ornamental grasses. Low growing shrubs such as *Deutzia* 'Nikko,' *Cotoneaster salicifolia* 'Rependans,' or the mounding Spireas such as *Spirea japonica* 'Limemound,' 'Little Princess,' or 'Shibori' are also good choices for ground covers in a sunny location.

Do you need a focal point? Plants work admirably for this purpose, when used individually for their own fascinating characteristics or grouped in attractive containers. My rule of focal points is—less is more. One special feature per area is adequate, two or three if they complement each other. More than once I have seen a lovely garden compromised by the addition of too many showy plants or a lot of small, distracting features spotted helter-skelter throughout the landscape.

After you have sketched out your plant needs, make a list. How many trees do you need and what size should they be at maturity? How many evergreens for screening? Do you need shrubs that are evergreen or deciduous, flowering specimens or background plantings? What are the dimensions of flower gardens and ground cover areas? Once you know what you need, you can determine the cultural conditions and space availability.

I encourage you to take the time to look up the botanical names—genus, species and cultivar—for your selections. Here is how it works. Genus applies to the group of plants to which it belongs, for example *Forsythia*. Within this group are many individual variations designated by species, for example *Forsythia intermedia*. The species name appears second and it is usually not capitalized unless it is named for a person or place. The cultivar is a plant selected or hybridized for special characteristics. It is given a special name, which is always enclosed by single quotation marks and capitalized, i.e. 'Lynwood Gold.' *Forsythia intermedia* 'Lynwood Gold' would be an upright, fast growing shrub up to nine feet high and wide, suitable for screening, and bearing bright golden yellow flowers in early spring. On the other hand, *Forsythia virridissima* 'Bronxiensis' is a twelve-inch tall spreading shrub, suitable as a ground cover, and bearing pale yellow flowers in early spring. It would be unfortunate to pick up a plant labeled *Forsythia* and get one that did not meet your expectations or your needs.

A problem with using common names is that they are not specific enough to assure you'll get the plant you want. In addition, the same common name may apply to different plants in different parts of the country. For example, in some places Japonica is the common name of flowering quince or *Chaenomeles speciosa*, a large deciduous shrub that grows in full sun. In other places the common name Japonica refers to *Pieris japonica*, a slow growing, evergreen shrub that thrives in shade. By arriving at the garden center armed with a specific list of botanical names, you will save time and money and end up with the landscape you envisioned. It's a small effort when you think of how many years you will live with your landscape.

Are there areas of your plan where you're not sure what you need? Don't hesitate to leave them open at first. As you see

Texture, color, screening, and seasonal interest are some of the many benefits plants provide.

the plan come together on the ground, you will be able to make better decisions about what, if any, plant to use. And you may see plants in magazines or other gardens that you simply must have. If you leave some open space in your landscape you can fit them in without over-planting.

Colorful foliage plants can be very dramatic and they have the advantage of providing a consistent effect throughout the growing season. Their color does not come and go, as is the case with most flowering plants. Brightly colored foliage can be a distraction, however, so use it with discretion. Both flowers and foliage color can be repeated to pull the composition together. Showy foliage can become a beacon, drawing the eye and disrupting the flow of lines through the landscape. If your intent is to draw attention to an area or feature, a bold splash of foliage color will do the trick. Just use it with care, or your vision will be bouncing all over the place.

Color Considerations

Color is a sensitive issue. I am very particular about color combinations in my garden. There are no hard and fast rules, however, because it is another matter of taste. I will set out some guidelines I use, and encourage you to do what pleases you. If my guidelines are helpful, that's good, but don't feel like they are cast in stone, even if I make them sound that way.

- Choose colors to reinforce the general theme of your garden.

  Pastels, cool colors, shades of green and white, and subtle use of color suit a quiet, restful space.

  Bright, hot colors and strong contrasts set a lively mood for active use areas.

- Warm colors, such as orange-red, yellow, and orange are easily seen at a distance.

- Cool colors such as blue, violet, and green tend to recede. Use them for close-up viewing.

- A bit of white can add sparkle to a color scheme. However, large blocks of white can punch holes in the garden composition.

- A garden designed in shades of white can be fascinating.

- Program the garden by choosing an attractive color combination for each season of bloom.

- Consider your interior color scheme when planting so that you can cut flowers from the garden for arrangements.

- Experiment with color by planting inexpensive annuals. When you find combinations that please you, duplicate them with perennials and shrubbery.

- Until you feel confident in combining colors, varying lighter and darker shades of the same color is most always attractive.

A color scheme in the garden will help you to maintain the continuity of style we have tried to achieve through design. My property is relatively large, so I have turned part of it into a meadow. I have chosen its color scheme from adjacent colors on the color wheel. In the meadow, gold, orange, and red flowers are scattered through the graceful, airy-textured grasses. I punch up this combination with touches of opposing colors—a bright cobalt blue and vibrant purple. Wow, that's not a color scheme for a timid soul! This combination might be too strong if used in concentrated blocks of flowers, but scattered among the greens and tans of summer grasses, it is lively and energetic, just the feeling I want for the meadow.

At another place on the property, visually isolated from the meadow, I have planted a long perennial border ending with a bench. Here, the color scheme changes through the seasons from hot pink, shades of mauve, and purples in spring, to pale pink, icy lavender, and white in the heat of summer. Silver foliage reinforces the frosty effect. I find this color scheme very light and cool in hot weather. The bench is a pleasant place to linger on warm evenings, surrounded by the fragrance of a multitude of flowers, watching the hummingbirds and butterflies dip down for a taste of nectar.

In a tree-shaded courtyard, I rely primarily on foliage texture and patterns of light and shade to add interest. In early spring, the delicate white daffodil 'Thalia' complements blue Virginia bluebells and rose-pink bleeding hearts. As they fade, masses of light violet iris bloom in late spring. Summer finds this garden full of contrasting shades of green with little or no flower color. Some years I add a flat of white impatiens spotted among the plants. The feeling I am trying to achieve here is cool, quiet, and serene and I don't want a lot of distracting color.

Color, as you see from these examples, can help your garden speak to you. Whether it will be a shout or a whisper is your choice. Whatever you decide upon, just be consistent. On my way home from work, I drive past a lovely landscape based on shades of yellow, white, and blue with foliage contrasts of rich dark and cool lime green. The house was sold recently and I drove by one day this past spring to see a bold red Japanese maple planted in the middle of the lawn. It was a distracting element and completely disrupted the pleasant harmony of the well-planned garden. Watch out for those strong color contrasts. They will punch holes in your carefully crafted design. Use color with care.

When designing your planting scheme, keep in mind the constant change that takes place in a garden. It is wonderful to have crocus, daffodils, and other flowering bulbs announce spring. Soon the next wave of flowers—tulips, iris, *dianthus*, bleeding hearts and more—begins to bloom. With a carefully programmed perennial garden, you can have flowers blooming throughout the spring, summer, and fall. Note that weather conditions can influence bloom time by as much as two weeks, however, so it is really more of an art than a science.

A garden is in a constant state of growth, decline, and renewal. Remember those spring bulbs—their foliage must be left to ripen so that they will bloom the following year, and it can be unsightly. Consider planting them in beds of perennials that will grow up and cover them as they fade. Predictable, seasonal changes can be planned for—the thrill of emerging life in spring, the pause in growth during the heat of summer, the beautiful ripeness of fall, the barren landscape of winter.

Think about capturing the quiet beauty of winter when you design your garden. This barren season extends over several months in our region—too long to be without garden pleasures! A balance of evergreen and deciduous material will provide seasonal interest and keep the garden from being completely denuded during the winter months. Evergreens enliven and warm the winter scene and are especially beautiful under a pristine blanket of snow.

Selections of *Viburnum*, crabapples, and hollies add the bright glow of berries to the fall and winter garden and attract birds that feed on them as their food supplies dwindle. Bird feeders attract a variety of feathered friends and keep the landscape lively. A heating element designed for the purpose will keep a pond from freezing over. Even containers that held masses of flowers all summer can be decorated for winter with evergreen and berried cutting. Be sure your containers are frost proof before leaving them outside.

There are less predictable changes as well. Sometimes a plant suffers an insect attack or a disease so virulent that it seems to curl up and die before your eyes. At times, you may not even be aware of the impending death until it's too late. In the case of disease, there is often no cure. I had two wonderful English walnut trees that screened my house from a busy road, gave me bushels of walnuts, and were beautiful shade trees. One spring, without warning, they leafed out very sparsely. An unusually wet summer had weakened them and a canker disease

had invaded them, shutting down their circulatory system and killing them in one season.

There is nothing to do in such cases but remove the ailing plant and replace it. It is useful to try to find out what caused the decline or death, however. For example, if excessive moisture was the culprit, you can improve drainage or make a new selection that is more tolerant of these conditions. I recommend choosing a plant from a different genus as a replacement, or the same factor that killed the first plant could attack the replacement.

A mature saucer magnolia is a striking focal point all year long. Its beauty begins with the stark silhouette of branches against a winter sky, evolves to the soft pink of spring blossoms, and then to rich dark green foliage during the rest of the season.

Trees are the backbone of a garden. They are a strong structural element that helps to align the scale of the architecture with its surroundings. Here, colorful beds of perennials and annuals glow against a backdrop of trees.

Shrub roses create a billowing informal hedge. Many new cultivars of roses flower throughout the growing season with very little care.

A lively green "wall" of Leyland cypress shields a residential property from view. Leyland cypress is an extremely fast growing evergreen, ideally suited for screening.

Ostrich ferns are an excellent ground cover for a partly sunny area. hosta, liriope, pachysandra, and vinca are all effective at reducing maintenance

A mass of perennials acts as a ground cover by crowding out most weed growth. If a few weeds do grow, they are only discernable by the knowledgeable horticulturist.

Blues and violets tend to recede in the field of vision, while reds and yellows come forward. When a garden is designed to be viewed from a distance, the warm colors are more effective.

An ancient Sycamore tree serves as a focal point in this composition.

This small fountain, located near a dining terrace, provides a charming focal point as well as a relaxing background sound.

A rose covered arbor creates a colorful entrance to a home vegetable garden.

A potager is an ornamental garden using flowers, herbs, and vegetables. This one is located in a barn ruin.

Vegetable plants can be used as ornamentals with additional benefits. This bush squash blooms exuberantly and produces plentiful summer squash for the table. The Savoy cabbage resembles a large green rose, a lovely accompaniment to flowering annuals.

A potager is often enclosed by a fence or hedge and intersected by paths, for ease of access to the beds.

Growing herbs and vegetables is a very satisfying hobby. There is nothing like a tomato fresh from the vine or sweet corn picked minutes from the pot.

Colorful foliage is a wonderful accent, and foliage color is more stable than flowers. This red threadleaf maple creates a focal point in a poolside garden.

A cool-hued summer garden relies on textures for excitement.

An oakleaf hydrangea in full bloom is a dramatic picture. This plant will grow eight to ten feet high and wide and its rangy form does not lend itself to extensive pruning. Mature size of plants is an important design consideration.

Flowing *Clematis montana* softens a porch. Vines are also useful for providing quick shade when grown on a pergola.

Plantings complement a small water feature
and make it part of the landscape.

Hollyhocks are at home against a barn door. Plants can reinforce the style of the landscape.

A well planned border has flowers in bloom from early spring to the heavy frosts of fall. In winter, seeds and stalks provide color and textural interest.

Plants in containers add drama and color right where they are needed. The containers in these pictures demonstrate very different styles. Each is suitable to the garden in which it is located.

Winter interest can come from bright
berries or the colorful peeling bark of these
Heritage river birches.

Appendix

Idea Pages

These pages are designed to stimulate your thinking by showing you some sample landscape features. They are not intended to be a comprehensive illustration of all possible alternatives—if that were the case, thousands of photos would be needed! Here you will find examples of real world solutions that people like you have used in developing landscapes they live in and enjoy. **Always check with local building codes before undertaking any landscape construction.**

Fences, Walls, and Enclosures

There are many reasons why you might want to enclose an area, and just as many ways to do it. If you wish to keep something or someone in or out, a fence is often the best choice. Fences are also used as ornamental enclosures to give a rustic or a historic appearance to a garden plot. They can be used for privacy as well.

Walls, like fences, can be used to enclose areas, screen for privacy, or serve a purely decorative function. Retaining walls are used to create level areas from sloping terrain or to ease grade changes. Walls can be constructed from wood, boulders, various types of stone, brick, interlocking pavers, or concrete block with a stucco finish. They may be capped with decorative copping, brick, slabs of cut stone, or molded concrete blocks—or they may be left uncapped. A wall of about eighteen inches in height, capped by smooth stone slabs, can be used as informal seating.

Plants provide another way of enclosing space. Fast growing shrubs such as those in the Viburnum genus will quickly grow together and screen an area. A neatly clipped hedge of lower growing Boxwood 'Winter Gem' or 'Green Beauty' will provide a boundary that defines an area without cutting off views. A mixed shrub border is an attractive way of enclosing large spaces. It can be very effective as a green wall, and with a selection of evergreen and flowering shrubbery the shrub border can provide year round interest as well as food and shelter for song birds.

Traditional white picket fence.

Iron fence.

Stucco over block wall with stone columns and cap.

Weathered wood fence.

Split rail fence with wire mesh.

Granite wall.

Barn ruin walls.

Seat wall.

Viburnum screen.

Mixed planting used for privacy.

Overhead Structures

There is something intrinsically appealing about an overhead structure. Whether it comes from a lattice-work arbor or a sturdy pergola, the sense of being enclosed and yet open to the surrounding landscape is very attractive. An overhead structure is a wonderful way to enhance architecture, support vines, and screen unattractive views. An arbor or pergola provides light shade instantly, and when planted with fast growing vines will create a cool hideaway from summer sun in much less time than it would take a young tree to provide comparable shade.

A simple arbor.

A shade structure.

Vines on an overhead structure.

Painted arbor.

An arched arbor.

Stucco columns support a pergola.

Underfoot

The surface underfoot serves multiple purposes. The first and foremost is to allow safe and easy walking through the landscape. The type of material and the size and shape of the paved area also contribute to the style or impression made by the landscape, the speed with which people move through it, and the level of maintenance required.

Poured concrete is widely used for walks, terraces, and driveways in the mid-Atlantic states. Concrete forms a smooth, firm surface. It can conform to a straight or curvilinear design and it needs limited maintenance. New dyed and stamped concrete applications allow for a wide variety of colors and surface textures. Concrete has its downside, however. I rarely see a concrete walk or slab over three years old that is without cracks. A good base, one that allows for drainage and supports the concrete, helps to maintain its integrity. Expansion joints are needed to allow for slight movement in response to freezing and thawing. Concrete is at great risk from the expansion and contraction caused by our constantly changing winter temperatures.

The surface of concrete can be stained by spills or an accumulation of leaves. It should be sealed for best appearance and will need to be resealed every couple of years, depending upon traffic. Salt used to melt ice and snow can erode the surface of concrete. Perhaps the biggest downside, however, is that of limited accessibility to cables or pipes installed beneath concrete. There is no way to reach them for repair or additions, except by cutting and removing the concrete, often requiring the whole installation to be replaced.

Paving made of brick or stone is often set in a mortar bed over a concrete base. This is a very attractive and low maintenance application. The concrete base should still be installed with proper base and expansion joints. However, the stone or brick will be much more attractive than a plain concrete surface and minor cracking will be hidden. This is a very serviceable, attractive, and long-lasting surface, although it shares with concrete the problem of accessing utilities that are beneath it. Restoration after cutting is possible, however, since the brick or stone will hide the patch.

A second type of paving is known as permeable or dry-laid paving because it allows moisture to pass through it. Examples of permeable paving are brick or concrete pavers set in a sand bed. Cut or natural stone can also be laid in this way. Loose gravel is another example of pervious paving materials. All of these applications have the advantage of being easily removed and reset if necessary. By allowing water infiltration, they reduce runoff problems. Their flexibility allows for slight movement as winter temperatures change, with no resulting damage.

Dry-laid paving will accommodate tree roots without damage to the pavement or the trees. In time, this type of pavement takes on a pleasantly irregular surface that goes well with a rustic or period style of architecture. Brick and stone and/or gravel can be combined for an interesting effect.

Mulch or wood chips are sometimes used in very casual settings to create paths. This is a high maintenance application and is best viewed as a temporary solution. Weeds quickly invade mulched areas as mulch breaks down, and as a traffic surface it requires frequent renewal. However, if there is a ready supply of inexpensive material it can be quite nice underfoot as a woodland path.

Wood decking and boardwalks are used less these days because of their high maintenance requirements and the relatively short lifespan of wood when exposed to the elements. The new composite woods are quite attractive and they may change that trend as they become more widely available and accepted. They are quite expensive right now, but appealing nonetheless for their appearance and low maintenance. One caution about wood surfaces—they are slippery when wet. A damp wood surface can be nearly as slick as ice and also tends to freeze before other surfaces. I would certainly avoid using wood for a primary entrance and would take measures to reduce the slip and fall risk wherever it is used.

Pea gravel path with Belgian Block and Bluestone paving.

Brick with Belgian block edging.

Bluestone terrace.

Pennsylvania antique stone slabs.

Brick and uncut Avondale flagstone.

Pea gravel path with hostas.

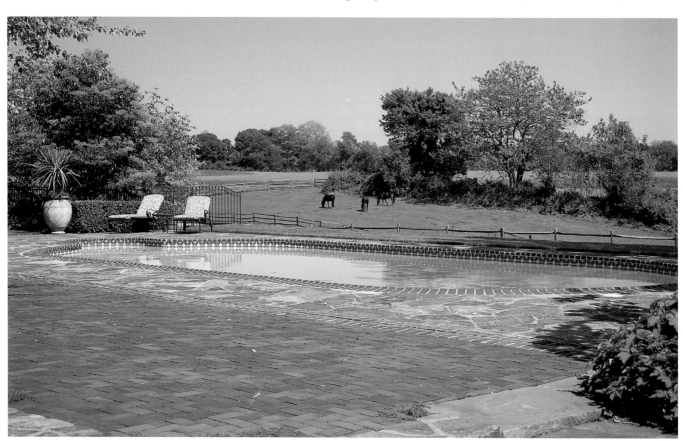

Brick main walk and stone secondary walk set in turf.

Rustic uncut stone walk.

Garden Accents

Just as written text needs punctuation, so do gardens. Punctuation help clarify meaning, control flow, and add interest to spoken and written words. In the garden, those benefits are derived from accent features such as columns, sculpture, fountains, containers, fences, walls, and hedges. The possibilities are endless. The important point is that the features chosen for this purpose should be complementary to the overall style of the landscape.

Column and brick edging accents.

An interesting birdbath stands at the junction of paths in a recreation of an historic garden style.

Container on column.

Container at junction of walks.

Stone detail
on column.

Colorful container at terrace entrance.

Container on porch.

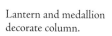
Lantern and medallion
decorate column.

Sculpture personalizes a garden.

Herbs in containers decorate the outdoor kitchen.

A decorative birdhouse.

Furnishings

Furnishings add functionality and comfort to the landscape. When selecting garden furniture, consider style, durability, comfort, and maintenance requirements.

Natural wood and wicker furniture must be protected from the weather. These materials are best used on an enclosed terrace or porch where they will not be exposed to the elements. They can be painted with a preservative to somewhat prolong their life out of doors.

Iron furniture will need periodic wire brushing and re-painting. Newer paint products are very durable in an outdoor setting, but will last longer if stored inside over winter or at least protected from the elements by a fitted cover. Cast aluminum furniture is an excellent choice for outdoor furnishings. It is carefree and durable and can stay in place year around—an important consideration for large pieces or where limited storage space is available. There are also some attractive synthetic materials on the market. You may need to do some comparison shopping to find the most suitable style and material for your particular situation.

Cast aluminum furniture.

Iron furniture.

Weathered wood furniture.

Wood benches built
into a deck.

Iron and synthetic
furniture.

A well furnished
pool deck.

Sizzle and Splash

Outdoor kitchens are becoming increasingly important as we view our landscapes as extensions of our homes. Enjoying outdoor activities at home has become a relaxing alternative to the stress and risks of travel. As our attention shifts to the home environment, swimming pools and decorative water features, including ponds, streams, waterfalls, and fountains, are finding a place in many gardens.

Fire pits and outdoor fireplaces are gaining in popularity as well. Brick and stone are the traditional materials for fireplaces and outdoor grills. These structures need to be built by a knowledgeable mason for reasons of safety and functionality.

Fire pits are new items on the landscape scene. They can be built into the landscape using a number of materials or they can be portable. The most successful ones are in a natural appearing setting and are made of materials that harmonize with the setting.

Chimeneas, fire bowls, and portable fireplaces are very popular and easy to use. They can be made of ceramic, copper, or cast iron. A spark screen is a must for safety, with any fireplace.

Top:
Pool house with kitchen.

Middle:
Grill built into stone wall adjacent to deck.

Bottom:
A new fire pit.

Outdoor fireplace.

Poolside grill.

Chiminea at poolside.

Small fountain near dining area.

Rectilinear reflecting pond on multilevel terrace.

Sculpture decorates a pond on a pea gravel terrace.

Waterfall with plantings.

Steps

Outdoor steps are necessary in many landscapes for transitioning from one grade to another. They require careful planning to be safe and attractive. Materials used are the same as those used for paving, and steps should coordinate with the surrounding pavements. If ramps are desired for handicapped accessibility, a registered landscape architect or civil engineer should be consulted.

Brick seating steps.

Stone slabs
with boulders.

Wood steps and deck.

Stone treads set into lawn create an informal grade transition and give definition to the space. The brick edging ties in with a nearby brick terrace.

Informal steps up a hillside.

Reliable Plants for the Mid-Atlantic Garden

Below is a brief list of my favorite plants. It is by no means a comprehensive list of desirable landscape plants, but includes those chosen for hardiness, attractiveness, and adaptability. I strongly encourage you to research each plant carefully before you decide to use it in your landscape. An excellent reference volume titled *Hardy Trees and Shrubs, An Illustrated Encyclopedia* has been compiled by Michael Dirr. While this is a valuable reference for any gardener, it is not specific to the Mid-Atlantic region.

Since I don't have unlimited garden space or resources, I ask a lot of each plant. From trees, I expect shade, hardiness, low maintenance, a size appropriate to the space and flower, foliage or decorative bark for interest in one or more seasons. My requirements for shrubs are similar. From perennials, I want ease of culture, dependability, and attractive flowers and foliage.

Some very popular plants do not make the cut in my garden. An example is butterfly bush (Buddelia cvs.). While attractive in bloom, this shrub's brown, faded flowers cling long after they are done blooming. Most people don't have the time to trim each successive wave of flowers, so I often see Buddelias covered with unattractive dead flowers.

This plant list is organized by trees, evergreen trees, shrubs, vines, and perennials, ferns, and grasses.

Trees

Botanical Name	Common Name
Acer griseum	Paperbark Maple
Acer palmatum	Japanese Maple
Acer rubrum 'Red Sunset'	'Red Sunset' Red Maple
Acer saccharum 'Legacy'	'Legacy' Sugar Maple
Acer saccharum 'Green Mountain'	'Green Mountain' Sugar Maple
Betula nigra 'Heritage'	'Heritage' River Birch
Cercidiphyllum japonica	Katsura Tree
Cornus kousa	Korean Dogwood
Cornus x 'Rutlan'	'Ruth Ellen' Hybrid Dogwood
Gleditsia triacanthos inemis 'Shademaster'	'Shademaster' Thornless Honeylocust
Halesia Carolina	Carolina Silverbells
Kolreuteria paniculata	Golden Rain Tree
Magolia acuminate 'Butterflies'	'Butterflies' Magnolia
Magnolia grandiflora	Southern Magnolia
Prunus subhirtella 'Autumnalis'	Autumn Blooming Cherry
Prunus subhirtella 'Pendula'	Weeping Cherry
Prunus yedoensis	Yoshino Cherry
Quercus alba	White Oak
Quercus phellos	Willow Oak
Quercus rubra	Red Oak
Sophora Japonica 'Regent'	Japanese Pagoda Tree
Stewartia pseudocamellia	Japanese Stewartia
Taxodium distichum	Bald or Swamp Cypress
Ulmus parvifolia 'Dynasty' or 'Allee'	'Dynasty' or 'Allee' Chinese Elm

Evergreen Trees

Botanical Name	Common Name
Cedrus Atlantica 'Glauca'	Blue Atlas Cedar
Cupressocyparis x. leylandii	Leyland Cypress
Ilex x aquipernyi 'San Jose'	San Jose Holly
Juniperus virginiana	Eastern Red Cedar
Picea Abies	Norway Spruce
Pinus strobus	Eastern White Pine
Pseudotsuga menziesii	Douglas Fir
Thuja occidentalis 'Emerald Green'	Emerald Green Arborvitae

Shrubs

Botanical Name	Common Name
Abelia grandiflora	Glossy Abelia
Abelia 'Edward Goucher'	'Edward Goucher' Abelia
Berberis thunbergia atropurpurea 'Nana'	'Crimson Pygmy' Barberry
Buxus microphylla koreana 'Winter Beauty'	'Winter Beauty' Boxwood
Buxus microphylla koreana 'Franklins Gem'	'Franklin's Gem' Boxwood
Buxus sempervirens	American Boxwood
Caryopteris x clandonensis 'Blue Mist'	'Blue Mist' Bluebeard
Caryopteris x clandonensis 'Longwood'	'Longwood Blue' Bluebeard
Chamaecyparis obtusa 'Gracilis' or 'Compacta'	Compact Hinoki Cypress
Cornus alba siberica	Red Twig Dogwood
Deutzia gracilis and 'Nikko'	Slender Deutzia & 'Nikko' Deutzia
Euonymus alatus 'Compact'	Compact Burning Bush
Hamamelis vernalis	Vernal Witch Hazel
Hamamelis x intermedia 'Arnold's Promise'	'Arnold's Promise' Witch Hazel
Hibiscus syriacus 'Bluebird', 'Diana'	'Bluebird' and 'Diana' Althea
Hydrangea panicula 'Tardiva'	Tardiva Hydrangea
Hydrangea serrata 'Blue Billow'	'Blue Billow' Hydrangea
Hydrangea quercifolia 'Snow Queen'	'Snow Queen' Oakleaf Hydrangea
Hydrangea quercifolia 'Alice'	'Alice Oakleaf' Hydrangea
Ilex crenata 'Helleri', 'Hoogendorn', 'Steeds'	'Helleri,' 'Hoogendorn,' and 'Steed's' Japanese Holly
Ilex glabra 'Compacta'	Compact Inkberry
Ilex verticillata 'Winter Red'	'Winter Red' Winterberry
Ilex x meserveae 'China Boy' 'China Girl'	'China Boy,' 'China Girl' Holly
Ilex x meserveae 'Blue Maid', 'Blue Princess'	'Blue Maid,' 'Blue Princess' Holly
Ilex x meserveae 'Blue Stallion'	'Blue Stallion' Holly
Rhododendron x 'PJM'	'PJM' Rhododendron
Rosa x 'Knockout', 'Pink Knockout', 'Blushing Knockout'	'Knockout' Roses
Spirea x vanhouttei	Vanhoutte Spirea
Syringa vulgaris hybrids	Common Lilac and hybrids
Taxus baccata 'Repandens'	Weeping English Yew
Viburnum carlesii	Fragrant Viburnum, Korean Spice Viburnum
Viburnum dentatum 'Blue Muffin'	'Blue Muffin' Arowwood Viburnum
Viburnum dilitatum & 'Michael Dodge'	Linden Viburnum and 'Michael Dodge' Linden Viburnum
Viburnum plicatum tomentosum 'Mariesii'	'Maries' Doublefile Viburnum

Vines

Botanical Name	Common Name
Campsis radicans 'Madam Galen'	'Madam Galen' Trumpet Vine
Clematis-large flowered cultivars	Clematis cvs.
Clematis montana and 'Rubens'	Montana Clematis, Pink Montana Clematis
Clematis paniculata	Sweet Autumn Clematis
Hydrangea anomala petiolaris	Climbing Hydrangea
Lonicera sempervirens	Honeysuckle

Perennials, Ferns, and Grasses

Botanical Name	Common Name
Adiantum pedatum	Maidenhair Fern
Achillea 'Coronation Gold'	'Coronation Gold' Yarrow
Achillea 'Red Beauty'	'Red Beauty' Yarrow
Aconitum 'Arendsii'	Monkshood
Alchemilla mollis	Lady's Mantle
Anemone japonica 'Queen Charlotte'	'Queen Charlotte' Japanese Anemone
Anemone japonica 'September Charm'	'September Charm' Japanese Anemone
Anemone japonica 'Whirlwind'	'Whirlwind' Japanese Anemone
Anemone sylvestris	Snowdrop Anemone
Artemesia 'Powis Castle', 'Silver King'	Wormwood
Athyrium Nipponicum 'Pictum'	Japanese Painted fern
Asclepias tuberosa	Butterfly Weed
Astilbe 'Ostrich Feather', 'Bridal Veil', 'Fanal'	'Ostrich Feather', 'Bridal Veil', and 'Fanal' False Spirea
Begonia grandis & 'Alba'	Hardy Begonia & White Hardy Begonia
Brunnera macrophylla	Heartleaf Brunnera
Campanula persicifolia	Peachleaved Bellflower
Campanula poscharskyana	Serbian Bellflower
Chrysanthemum indicum 'Sheffield Pink'	'Sheffield Pink' Chrysanthemum
Dianthus cvs.	Garden Pinks, Dianthus
Dicentra spectabilis & 'Alba'	Bleeding Heart & White Bleeding Heart
Digitalis grandiflora	Perennial Foxgloves
Digitalis purpurea	Foxgloves
Dryopteris marginalis	Evergreen Wood Fern
Gallium odoratum	Sweet Woodruff
Geranium cvs.	Hardy Geranium, Cranesbill
Gysophila 'Festival White' or 'Festival Pink'	Baby's Breath or Pink Baby's Breath
Helleborus niger or *orientalis*	Lenten Rose or Christmas Rose
Hemerocallis cvs	Daylily
Heuchera cvs	Coral Bells
Hosta cvs	Hosta
Iris Siberica 'Caesar's Brother'	'Caesar's Brother' Siberian Iris
Iris Siberica 'Snow Queen'	'Snow Queen' Siberian Iris
Liriope muscari 'Big Blue' and others	'Big Blue' Lilyturf
Lysamachia nummularia 'Aurea'	Golden Creeping Jenny
Matteuccia struthiopteris	Ostrich Fern
Miscanthus sinensis 'Gracillimus', 'Morning Light'	Maiden Grass, 'Morning Light' Maiden Grass
Oenethera tetragona 'Fireworks'	Sundrops
Osmunda cinnamomea	Cinnamon Fern
Paeonia lactiflora	Garden Peony
Paeonia suffruticosa	Tree Peony
Panicum virgatum 'Shenandoah'	'Shenandoah' Switch Grass
Papaver orientale	Oriental Poppy
Pennesitum alopecuroides 'Karley Rose'	'Karley Rose' Fountain Grass
Penstemon 'Husker's Red' and others	'Husker's Red' Beard Tongue
Perovskia atriplicifolia 'Filigran'	'Filigran' Russian Sage
Platycodon grandiflorus 'Mariesii'	'Marie's' Balloon Flower
Polystichum acrostichoides	Christmas Fern
Rudbeckia fulgida var. 'Goldstrum'	'Goldstrum' Black-eyed Susan
Sedum 'Autumn Joy' and many others	'Autumn Joy' Sedum
Thymus serpyllum coccineus and others	Scarlet Thyme
Vernonia novaboracensis	Ironweed

Daylilies are a reliable and colorful perennial.

An oakleaf hydrangea is a striking specimen.

Pennesitum 'Karley Rose'.

A hydrangea lights up
a shaded corner.

The colorful foliage of a threadleaf Japanese maple.

References

Natural Gardens

Darke, Rick. *The American Woodland Garden*. Oregon: Timber Press, 2002.

Druse, Ken. *The Natural Garden*. New York: Clarkson N. Potter, Inc, 1992.

Kingsbury, Joel. *Natural Gardening in Small Spaces*. Oregon: Timber Press, 1996.

Kingsbury, Joel. *The New Perennial Garden*. New York: Henry Holt and Company, 1996.

Oudolf, Piet and Henk Gerritsen. *Planting the Natural Garden*. Oregon: Timber Press, 2003 (English edition).

Van Sweden, James. *Bold Romantic Gardens*. Australia: Florilegium, 1998.

Van Sweden, James. *Gardening with Nature*. New York: Random House, 1997. 2003.

Garden Style

Baker, Martha. *The Outdoor Living Room*. New York: Clarkson, Potter/Publishers, 2001.

Jones, Louisa. *Le Nouvel Esprit des Jardins*. France: Hachette Livre, 1998.

Water Gardens

Archer-Wills, Anthony. *The Water Gardener*. London: Baron's Educational Series Ltd., 1993.

Van Sweden, James. *Gardening With Water*. New York: Random House, 1995.

Color Theory

Good, Jane, Ed. *The Gardeners Color Guide*. New York, Ontario: Camden House Publishing, 1993.

Harper, Pamela, J. *Color Echoes*. New York: Macmillan Publishing, 1994.

Pruning

Hill, Lewis. *Pruning Made Easy: A Gardener's Visual Guide to When and How to Prune Everything, from Flowers to Trees*. Canada: Transcontinental Printing, 1997.

Plant References

Dirr, Michael. *Hardy Trees and Shrubs: An Illustrated Encyclopedia*. Oregon: Timber Press, Inc., 1997.

Rice, Graham, and Kurt Bluemel. *Encyclopedia of Perennials*. New York: DK Publishing Inc., 2006.

Public and Private Gardens

Levine, Adam, and Rob Cardillo. *A Guide to the Great Gardens of the Philadelphia Region*. Philadelphia: Temple University Press, 2007.

The Garden Conservancy's Open Days Directory: A Guide to Visiting America's Best Private Gardens. Cold Spring, New York: The Garden Conservancy, 2005.

Index